Excursions

❖

Number Two

A Prime Puzzle

Dirichlet's theorem on primes in
arithmetic progressions

Martin Griffiths

The United Kingdom Mathematics Trust

A Prime Puzzle

© 2012 United Kingdom Mathematics Trust

All rights reserved. No part of this publication may be reproduced or transmitted in any form or by any means, electronic or mechanical, including photocopy, recording, or any information storage and retrieval system, without permission in writing from the publisher.

Published by The United Kingdom Mathematics Trust.
School of Mathematics, University of Leeds,
Leeds, LS2 9JT, United Kingdom
http://www.ukmt.org.uk

First published 2012.

ISBN 978-1-906001-16-2

Printed in the UK for the UKMT by Charlesworth Press, Wakefield.
http://www.charlesworth.com

Typographic design by Andrew Jobbings of Arbelos.
http://www.arbelos.co.uk

Typeset with LaTeX.

The books published by the United Kingdom Mathematics Trust are grouped into series.

❖

The EXCURSIONS IN MATHEMATICS series consists of monographs which focus on a particular topic of interest and investigate it in some detail, using a wide range of ideas and techniques. They are aimed at high school students, undergraduates and others who are prepared to pursue a subject in some depth, but do not require specialised knowledge.
1. *The Backbone of Pascal's Triangle*, Martin Griffiths
2. *A Prime Puzzle*, Martin Griffiths

❖

The HANDBOOKS series is aimed particularly at students at secondary school who are interested in acquiring the knowledge and skills which are useful for tackling challenging problems, such as those posed in the competitions administered by the UKMT and similar organisations.
1. *Plane Euclidean Geometry: Theory and Problems*, A D Gardiner and C J Bradley
2. *Introduction to Inequalities*, C J Bradley
3. *A Mathematical Olympiad Primer*, Geoff C Smith
4. *Introduction to Number Theory*, C J Bradley

❖

The PATHWAYS series aims to provide classroom teaching material for use in secondary schools. Each title develops a subject in more depth and in more detail than is normally required by public examinations or national curricula.
1. *Crossing the Bridge*, Gerry Leversha
2. *The Geometry of the Triangle*, Gerry Leversha

❖

The PROBLEMS series consists of collections of high-quality and original problems of Olympiad standard.
1. *New Problems in Euclidean Geometry*, David Monk

❖

The YEARBOOKS series documents all the UKMT activities, including details of all the challenge papers and solutions, lists of high scorers, accounts of the IMO and Olympiad training camps, and other information about the Trust's work during each year.

Contents

Series Editor's Foreword ... vii

Preface ... ix

Aims, motivation and mathematical prerequisites ... xi

I Setting the scene ... 1
1 A brief historical background to the problem ... 3
2 The Fundamental Theorem of Arithmetic ... 11
3 Summing the reciprocals of the primes ... 17

II The toolkit ... 23
4 Arithmetic functions ... 25
5 Limits and 'big oh' notation ... 35
6 Groups ... 43
7 The roots of unity ... 53
8 An introduction to characters ... 59
9 Dirichlet characters and their orthogonality relations ... 65
10 Dirichlet L-functions ... 75
11 The Möbius and Mangoldt functions ... 83
12 The generalised Möbius inversion formula ... 91

III The proof — **101**

13 The road map — 103
14 Estimating some sums — 109
15 The extraction process — 119
16 Rearranging a sum — 123
17 Showing that L_m is not zero — 129
18 The final step — 137
19 Afterword — 143

Appendices — **151**

A Convergent sequences and series — 153
B Proof by contradiction — 159
C Modular arithmetic — 161
D Complex numbers — 165
E Double sums — 169

Notation — 173
Hints to the challenges — 175
Answers and hints to the exercises — 187

Bibliography — 211
Index — 215

Series Editor's Foreword

This book is part of a series whose aim is to provide young mathematicians with a chance to engage with a topic in mathematics which is of particular interest to the author. The subject is explored both at length and in depth. At length: the ideas are followed along various paths to see how far they will go and to reveal connections between different parts of mathematics. In depth: the mathematical argument is treated rigorously and difficult steps are carefully explained in a way which is accessible to sixth-form students.

Another feature of the series is that much of the work is left to the reader in the form of exercises, challenges, tasks and research activities. This emphasizes the fact that reading mathematics is an active rather than a passive experience. The satisfaction in understanding challenging ideas is proportional to the effort made in doing so.

I hope that every secondary school will have these books in its library. The prices have been set so low that many good students will wish to purchase their own copies. Schools wishing to give out large numbers of copies of these books as prizes should note that discounts may be negotiated with the UKMT office.

Both the author and I would like to thank Nick Lord for the substantial contribution he has made to this book as principal referee.

London, UK   GERRY LEVERSHA

About the Author

Martin Griffiths joined the teaching profession following a career in the British Army. After completing his PGCE at the University of Nottingham, he started teaching mathematics at a large London comprehensive school. Martin was next appointed Head of Mathematics at a grammar school in Colchester, during which time he started writing about mathematics and completed both a part-time masters and a part-time doctorate in mathematics.

After fourteen thoroughly enjoyable years as a teacher, Martin took the plunge and entered the realms of Higher Education. He has held the posts of Lecturer in Mathematics Education at the University of Manchester and Lecturer in Mathematics at the University of Essex, and now works at the Mathematical Institute, University of Oxford.

Preface

The prime numbers 2, 3, 5, 7, ... are the building blocks of our number system. They have been studied for over 2000 years, but many mysteries remain. For example, we still do not know whether every even number greater than or equal to 4 is a sum of two prime numbers (Goldbach's conjecture), or whether there are infinitely many pairs of primes differing by 2 (the twin prime conjecture).

That having been said, the last two millennia have brought some successes, and this book is about one of the most spectacular, Dirichlet's theorem on primes in arithmetic progressions. It is obvious that there is only one prime which leaves a remainder of 3 on division by 9, namely 3 itself, since all such numbers are divisible by 3. Similarly there are no primes which leave a remainder of 10 on division by 95, all such numbers being multiples of 5. But are there infinitely many primes leaving a remainder of 7 on division by 9? What about primes leaving a remainder of 8 when divided by 11?

Dirichlet's famous theorem, proved 150 years ago, asserts that the answer to questions of this type is always "yes, unless there is some obvious reason why not". More precisely, there are infinitely many primes leaving a remainder of r on division by q if, and only if, r and q have no common factor greater than 1. Thus there are indeed infinitely many primes leaving a remainder of 7 on division by 9, and also infinitely many primes leaving a remainder of 8 on division by 11.

This book gives a comprehensive account of all the mathematics required to understand a proof of this theorem. It is designed to be read by highly motivated school students and offers a selection of material that is rather different from what might be termed the "Olympiad syllabus". Students can learn about the important functions of number theory, the very useful O-notation, a little group theory, some basic notions of analysis (limits and convergence) and a little bit of discrete Fourier analysis, even if they do not pursue the book all the way to the end. It offers good preparation for, but does not overlap excessively with, the first two years of an undergraduate course in mathematics. There are a number of enlightening historical remarks.

Dirichlet's theorem marked the birth of "analytic" number theory, leading eventually to the proof of the prime number theorem and the formulation of the Riemann hypothesis (one of the million dollar Clay Millenium problems). It introduced the mysterious objects called L-functions, which are central to much of modern number theory (such as the Birch and Swinnerton-Dyer conjecture, worth another million dollars) and which feature quite heavily in this book. Most students see little of either topic until well into an undergraduate course, if then, and a book attempting to remedy this situation is to be warmly welcomed.

Cambridge, UK   BEN GREEN

Ben Green is a Fellow of the Royal Society, and the Herchel Smith Professor of Pure Mathematics at the University of Cambridge.

Aims, motivation and mathematical prerequisites

The primary aim of this book is to present a proof of a truly magnificent theorem from the realms of number theory, a proof that can be understood by any able and determined person possessing post-16 mathematical knowledge. Indeed, the intended readership encompasses sixth-form students, undergraduates, teachers, lecturers or in fact anyone with a genuine interest in mathematics and a fascination for numbers in particular. As will become clear, however, beyond this primary aim lie a number of less explicit goals.

The reader might well ask why I chose *Dirichlet's theorem on primes in arithmetic progressions* on which to base an educational book on mathematics; why not something else? There are a number of reasons. First, it is a theorem requiring a 'large-scale' proof, and is thus suitable for a major project, thereby encouraging a holistic view of mathematics. It incorporates a wealth of beautiful mathematical ideas and arguments, and allows us to establish and to utilise some fascinating links between number theory, group theory, complex numbers, series and various arithmetic functions. It is also feasible to provide a stand-alone proof of the theorem for someone whose mathematical background does not go beyond pre-university mathematics. In short, it leads to work that is demanding yet accessible, aesthetically pleasing and wonderfully interconnected.

Over the years several proofs of Dirichlet's theorem have emerged. The one on which this book is based uses what mathematicians call 'elementary methods'. Please do not get the wrong idea here; 'elementary' in this context does *not* mean 'easy'. It simply means that the proof does not use elements from complex function theory. There are certainly briefer arguments employing complex-analytic ideas, but a vast amount of preparatory study in this area would be required in order to appreciate such proofs.

This book has been organised into three parts.

Part I: Setting the scene introduces the problem, gives some historical background and provides you with the chance to tackle some introductory material related to Dirichlet's theorem.
Part II: The toolkit gradually builds up the mathematical knowledge and skills required in order to follow a rigorous proof of the theorem.
Part III: The proof is the proof itself.

This structure allows for a fairly flexible approach to learning, and it is not necessary to read all of the chapters in sequence. You might want to dip into some of the later ones before returning to fill in details in earlier chapters. Indeed, this book will allow you to take a rambling, non-sequential approach to your studies, providing you with the opportunity to place some of the individual results in a broader context, thereby enabling the 'bigger picture' gradually to reveal itself. I very much believe that this is necessary in order to acquire genuine understanding of deep theorems. It is not crucial that every little step is understood immediately, so long as there is an appreciation of how it fits into the grand scheme of things. As a health warning, please note that not all of the preparatory work will be easy. In particular, some might find that the material in chapters 9 and 12 gives rise to a few sleepless nights.

Throughout the book there will be plenty of opportunities for readers actually to do some mathematics, so that they are very much engaged in the whole process rather than passive; after all, the only real way to learn mathematics is to get involved.

Challenges Scattered throughout the chapters are various challenges. These are intended to facilitate further immersion in the mathematics and occasionally to encourage exploration beyond the immediate area of interest. Hints are provided at the back of the book, but it is important to persevere with each problem before resorting to these.
Research activities The suggested research activities will allow broadening of mathematical horizons, particularly with regard to the history of mathematics. It is to be hoped that these snippets will whet the appetite sufficiently to initiate some independent reading.

Aims, motivation and mathematical prerequisites xiii

Exercises The exercises at the end of some chapters allow us to gain familiarity with, and an understanding of, the new material. The questions are roughly graded so that each exercise starts with easy problems and finishes with harder ones, some of which are not by any means straightforward.

Towards the back of the book can also be found ideas for further reading and a bibliography.

With regard to the presentation of the results in this book, a few theorems do appear in the early chapters just to maintain some sort of order at the outset. Later on, however, there are so many intermediate results that it is far more convenient simply to number them where they appear, as opposed to labelling them as individual lemmas or theorems. Besides, this more fluid approach serves to emphasise the vast web of mathematical interconnections comprising our proof of Dirichlet's theorem. It is possible, since there is so much going on in the proof, that periods of significant progress will be punctuated by phases of apparent stagnation associated with trying to keep in mind a wide range of new ideas at once. Indeed, mathematical endeavour can make us feel elated one minute and totally frustrated the next. However, it can all be absorbed and understood with a little patience and perseverance, and such mental struggles are part of the process of developing as a mathematician.

In order to prove Dirichlet's theorem we need to work in considerable generality. Most people, however, find the jump from the specific to the general rather difficult. Therefore, initially at least, many worked numerical examples are provided in order to illustrate the key mathematical ideas. Then, very gradually, these concrete examples disappear until there is hardly a number in sight.

As far as prior knowledge is concerned, we assume that the reader is familiar with mathematical ideas generally introduced in post-16 courses. Indeed, this book is essentially self-contained provided that the reader has some knowledge of the following mathematical topics: the definition of a logarithm (noting that we use $\log x$ to denote $\log_e x$ or $\ln x$ throughout), the laws of logarithms, summation notation, simple results on sequences and series (including the sum to infinity of a geometric progression), the binomial theorem, introductory calculus, the notion of a function, complex numbers in Cartesian form and proof by induction. Only a rudimentary knowledge of complex numbers is assumed, and we expand upon this somewhat in chapter 7 in order to ensure that the key points relevant to the proof of Dirichlet's theorem are understood. Finally, some knowledge of elementary number theory is assumed, as covered in the UKMT publication [3].

Part I

Setting the scene

Chapter 1

A brief historical background to the problem

I apologise for the pun in the title of this book, but it is indeed very apt. We are going to prove one of the truly great theorems of mathematics, one that is very much a prime puzzle about the prime numbers. The long and incredibly rich mathematical journey towards the solution of this demanding puzzle does not actually start until chapter 2. The purpose of the current chapter is merely to provide some historical background and to draw you into this fascinating problem. Do not be too concerned, therefore, if there are things in the next few pages that you do not follow entirely. All will be revealed by the time we get to the end of this book.

To start off with, I would like you to pick any two positive whole numbers, a and b. Now form the arithmetic progression given by

$$an + b, \quad n = 0, 1, 2, \ldots.$$

For example, if you chose $a = 7$ and $b = 8$ then your arithmetic progression would be $8, 15, 22, 29, \ldots$. Now consider the following question:

"Are there infinitely many primes in your arithmetic progression?"

To get a feel for the problem it might be an idea to start by writing out a few terms to see how the primes are distributed along the resulting arithmetic progression:

$8, 15, 22, \mathbf{29}, 36, \mathbf{43}, 50, 57, 64, \mathbf{71}, 78, 85, 92, 99, 106, \mathbf{113}, \ldots$

As indicated, the primes appearing so far are 29, 43, 71 and 113. They seem to be getting further apart as we go along the progression. Will this always be the case? By going 2 terms beyond 113 you will find the answer to this question. Besides, even if the primes were getting further apart, this would not necessarily tell us anything about the number of them in the arithmetic progression.

It turns out that the difficulty in deciding whether or not there are infinitely many primes in an arithmetic progression is highly dependent upon the choice of a and b. If you had chosen $a = 9$ and $b = 12$, for example, then the sequence $12, 21, 30, 39, 48, \ldots$ would have been generated, in which case the answer to my question is in the negative. It is indeed clear that this will always be the answer when a and b have a prime factor in common. Let us agree then to pick only values of a and b that are *coprime*. In other words, from now on we will consider only sequences of the form $\{an + b : n = 0, 1, 2, \ldots\}$, where a and b have no factors in common apart from 1.

A particularly simple case to look at under this restriction is $a = 2$ and $b = 1$, which gives the sequence of odd numbers:

$$1, 3, 5, 7, 9, 11, \ldots.$$

It is possible that you already know the answer to my question for this arithmetic progression, but if not then have a think about it before reading any further. It may have occurred to you that since $1, 3, 5, 7, \ldots$ contains all of the prime numbers except for 2 then we just need to decide whether or not there are infinitely many primes. Over 2000 years ago, Euclid proved that there are. He did this by assuming that there are only finitely many primes and, as a consequence of this assumption, arriving at a contradiction. If there are exactly k prime numbers, for some positive integer k, they can be listed as $p_1, p_2, \ldots p_k$, where $p_1 = 2$, $p_2 = 3$, and so on. Euclid then went on to form the number N that was one more than the product of all these primes:

$$N = p_1 p_2 \cdots p_k + 1.$$

By assumption, the prime factors of N come from the list $p_1, p_2, \ldots p_k$. However, each of these numbers leaves a remainder of 1 on dividing N, showing that not one of them could be a factor of N. Thus our initial assumption that there are only finitely many primes has led to nonsense, called a *contradiction*. We are forced to conclude, therefore, that

Chapter 1: A brief historical background to the problem

this assumption was not valid and that there are infinitely many primes. Incidentally, this particular method of proof, called *proof by contradiction*, will be employed several times throughout this book; for those that are unfamiliar with it, see appendix B.

So far then we have shown that the arithmetic progression with nth term $2n+1$ contains infinitely many primes. It is almost as straightforward to show that there are infinitely many primes of the form $4n+3$. To do this, start by assuming that there are exactly m such primes, $q_1, q_2, \ldots q_m$, where $q_1 = 3$, $q_2 = 7$, and so on. Now form the number

$$N = 4q_1 q_2 \cdots q_m - 1.$$

It is clear that N is not divisible by any of the m primes of the form $4n+3$. Thus, since N is odd, all its prime factors are of the form $4n+1$. However, the product of any set of integers, all of which are of the form $4n+1$, is also a number of this form; you should satisfy yourself that this is in fact true. This contradicts the fact that N is of the form $4n+3$, and it may be concluded from this that there are infinitely primes of the form $4n+3$. Since numbers of the form $4n+3$ are all of the form $2n+1$, this implies the previous result that there are infinitely primes of the form $2n+1$.

There are many other special cases that can be dealt with by employing various number-theoretical devices, and indeed some of these are mentioned in chapter 19. There is also a relatively straightforward way of showing that there are infinitely primes of the form $kn+1$ for any positive integer k. However, even this result is not entirely general since it does not tell us about the cases in which b is not equal to 1. Mathematicians always like to strive for results that are as general as possible, and this is our quest here.

Anyone wishing to know the answer to my initial question need not read any further than the following sentence, which is a statement of *Dirichlet's Theorem on Primes in Arithmetic Progressions*:

> The arithmetic progression given by $\{an+b : n = 0, 1, 2, \ldots\}$, where a and b are positive integers, contains infinitely many primes if, and only if, a and b are coprime.

However, the real challenge in mathematics lies in trying to understand why an answer is as it is. Therefore the principal aim of this book is to enable you to answer my initial question with complete confidence for any choice of a and b, whilst appreciating the mathematical ideas that go into justifying your answer. Here is a nice easy challenge to set you on your way:

Challenge 1.1 Is it ever possible for *all* the terms in the arithmetic progression given by $\{an + b : n = 0, 1, 2, \dots\}$ to be prime? Provide a clear justification of your answer.

It might be argued that Dirichlet's theorem had its origins in Euclid's proof of the infinitude of primes, over two millennia ago. While this may be true in some sense, the mathematics that Dirichlet required to prove his theorem was in a completely different league, incorporating and extending modern ideas and techniques developed by the famous Swiss mathematician Leonhard Euler (1707–1783).

In 1737 Euler came up with an alternative proof of the fact that there are infinitely many primes by studying the series consisting of the sum of their reciprocals,

$$\frac{1}{2} + \frac{1}{3} + \frac{1}{5} + \frac{1}{7} + \frac{1}{11} + \frac{1}{13} + \frac{1}{17} + \cdots,$$

and showing that this series diverges [15]. Of course, if there were only finitely many primes then the above series would converge; see appendix A for definitions of divergence and convergence. As you can imagine, this proof is considerably more involved than Euclid's. Some might wonder, therefore, why Euler went to the trouble of proving, by a more complicated method, something that had already been known for two millennia. Well, Euler was one of the truly great mathematicians, and possessed amazing mathematical insight. He realised his result, concerning the divergence of the sum of the reciprocals of the primes, tells us more than simply the number of primes is infinite. It also gives us some information about the density of the primes. It is known, for example, that the series consisting of the sum of the reciprocals of the non-zero square numbers converges. In fact, we have the following beautiful result, due to Euler:

$$\frac{1}{1^2} + \frac{1}{2^2} + \frac{1}{3^2} + \frac{1}{4^2} + \cdots = 1 + \frac{1}{4} + \frac{1}{9} + \frac{1}{16} + \cdots$$
$$= \frac{\pi^2}{6}. \tag{1.1}$$

You can find fourteen separate proofs of result (1.1) in the survey [13], and might find it worthwhile looking at some of these. Since there are also infinitely many square numbers, we cannot strictly say that result (1.1) concerning the sum of their reciprocals means that there are fewer squares than primes. It is possible, however, to infer from this that the primes are denser in the set of all integers than the squares. Roughly interpreted, this means that if we were to count the number of squares and the number of primes over a reasonably large interval of integers, from 5 000 000 to 6 000 000 for example, then we would expect there to be more primes than squares.

This work of Euler's led to all sorts of deep results concerning the theory of how prime numbers are distributed amongst the integers, with significant contributions from Adrien-Marie Legendre (1752–1833), Carl Friedrich Gauss (1777–1855), Johann Peter Gustav Lejeune Dirichlet (1805–1859), Pafnuty Lvovich Chebyshev (1821–1894), Bernhard Riemann (1826–1866) and Charles de la Vallée Poussin (1866–1962) amongst others. An excellent semi-popular account of this is given in [5].

It is, of course, the part played by Dirichlet that we are interested in here. He wanted to prove a corresponding result to Euler's, namely that if one sums the reciprocals of the primes in the arithmetic progression given by $\{an + b : n = 0, 1, 2, \ldots\}$, where a and b are coprime, then this series diverges, implying the infinitude of primes in this progression (as had been conjectured by both Gauss and Legendre). Dirichlet managed to achieve this feat, and his proof [9] was published in 1837. His analytic approach was ingenious; in fact this is considered by many to be the point at which an area of mathematics known as analytic number theory was born.

Dirichlet's original 1837 proof was rather complicated, however, and simplified versions were later given by other mathematicians. The proof in [1], on which we are basing the work in this book, was itself based on a proof by Harold Shapiro [18], published in 1952. As you will see, instead of, as Dirichlet did, looking at a series whose terms are all reciprocals of primes, Shapiro considered a series with terms of the form

$$\frac{\log p}{p},$$

where $\log x$ denotes the *natural logarithm* of x. It might seem strange that a series with more complicated looking terms can be more amenable analytically, but, as in other aspects of life, looks can be deceiving.

We now present a few interesting snippets of historical information about Dirichlet. If you would like a more in-depth account of his life and achievements then the webpage [21] is certainly worth visiting.

(a) You might think, by the sound of his surname, that Dirichlet was French. In actual fact he was German, born in the town of Düren near Cologne. Dirichlet's family originally came from Richelet in Belgium, from which his surname Lejeune Dirichlet was derived; the translation of "Le jeune de Richelet" being "Young man from Richelet".

(b) He had developed a passion for mathematics by the time he was 12 years old and spent much of his pocket-money on mathematics books! A comment on one of his school reports read " ... an unusually attentive and well-behaved pupil who was particularly interested in history as well as mathematics."

(c) Dirichlet had already acquired the qualifications necessary for university entrance by the time he was 16. He went to study in Paris, where he attended lectures by Fourier, Laplace, Legendre and Poisson amongst others. Dirichlet contracted smallpox while at university, but this did not keep him away from his lectures for long!

(d) Dirichlet's first paper, published in 1825, brought him immediate fame since it concerned the famous Fermat's Last Theorem (which was not actually a theorem at all until very recently). It was such a difficult problem to crack that mathematicians contented themselves with proving special cases. Dirichlet's paper partially dealt with the case $n = 5$. He later went on to prove the $n = 14$ case.

(e) He was appointed as a professor at the University of Berlin, and retained this post from 1828 to 1855. Here are two slightly contrasting excerpts from quotes concerning Dirichlet's character and teaching qualities:

"He was an excellent teacher, always expressing himself with great clarity. His manner was modest."

"He was unwashed, with his cup of coffee and cigar. One of his failings is forgetting time, he pulls his watch out, finds it past three, and runs out without even finishing the sentence."

(f) In 1831 Dirichlet married Rebecca Mendelssohn. She was a sister of the composer Felix Mendelssohn.

(g) In 1837, the same year in which he published his paper on primes in arithmetic progressions, Dirichlet was credited with proposing the

Chapter 1: A brief historical background to the problem   9

   modern definition of a function.
(h) He suffered a heart attack in 1858. Unfortunately, soon after this his wife died from a stroke. Dirichlet himself died the following year.

Research activity 1.1   Visit the website [22] in order to find out a bit more about some of the characters mentioned in this chapter. I, for one, feel that it is important to know something about where the mathematics that we use today comes from. You will find some of the potted biographies fascinating; I hope that this might inspire you to carry out some further reading on the historical aspect of mathematics.

Chapter 2

The Fundamental Theorem of Arithmetic

Dirichlet's theorem is essentially concerned with 'counting' prime numbers in an arithmetic progression. It is therefore first necessary to have a sound understanding of the basic multiplicative structure of the integers since primes are indeed defined in terms of this structure. A theorem of major importance in this regard is the *Fundamental Theorem of Arithmetic*. Even if you have never heard of this theorem before, you will almost certainly have met at least some aspects of it. It is concerned with the possibility of expressing positive integers as products of prime numbers. As the name of the theorem implies, most number-theoretic results depend on it.

We all learn at school how to express any positive integer $n > 1$ as a product of prime numbers. One nice visual method of doing this is by using a 'factor tree', in which the primes all finish up at the ends of the branches. Let us, for example, express 6650 as a product of primes. A factor tree for this is shown in figure 2.1. From this it can be seen that

$$6650 = 5 \times 2 \times 7 \times 5 \times 19$$
$$= 2 \times 5^2 \times 7 \times 19,$$

which is known as the *prime factorisation* of 6650 (it is sometimes also termed the *prime decomposition*). An alternative factor tree for 6650 is given in figure 2.2.

Note that although the factor tree in figure 2.2 looks rather different from the one in figure 2.1, both in terms of its shape and the numbers

```
              6650
           /        \
         50          133
        /  \        /   \
       5   10      7    19
           / \
          2   5
```
Figure 2.1

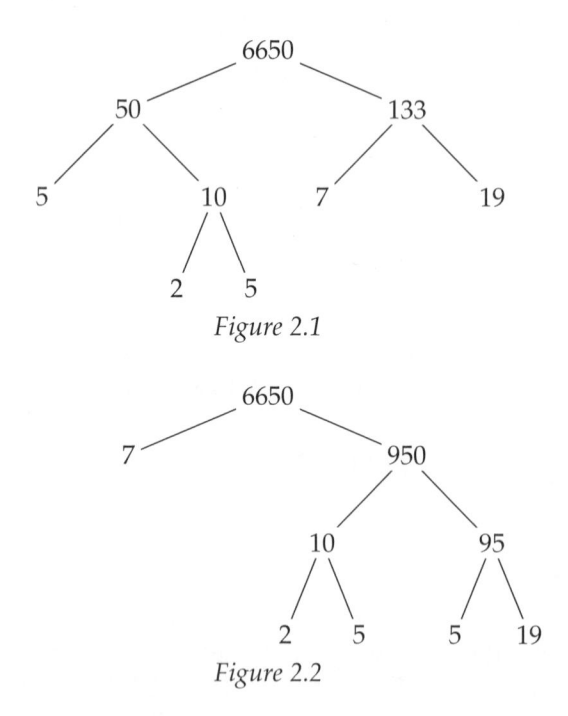

```
              6650
           /        \
          7          950
                    /    \
                  10      95
                 /  \    /  \
                2    5  5   19
```
Figure 2.2

appearing in the middle of the tree, the numbers at the ends of the branches are the same, albeit in different positions. The Fundamental Theorem of Arithmetic tells us that this will always the case. The primes, as a consequence of this, may be regarded as the basic building blocks of the multiplicative structure of the integers. We now state and prove the theorem, noting that $m \mid n$ and $m \nmid n$ are used to denote that m is and is not a factor of n, respectively.

Theorem 2.1 *Let n be any positive integer such that $n \geq 2$. Then n may be expressed a product of primes, and the resultant prime factorisation is unique up to the order of the factors.*

PROOF We proceed by induction on n. First, as base step, we note that the statement of the theorem is certainly true for $n = 2$. Let us now assume that it is true for all positive integers n satisfying $2 \leq n \leq k$ for some $k \geq 2$.

If $k+1$ is prime then the theorem is true for all n satisfying $2 \leq n \leq k+1$. Let us suppose, therefore, that $k+1$ is a composite number. Then

Chapter 2: The Fundamental Theorem of Arithmetic

$k+1 = ab$, where $2 \leq a, b \leq k$, and by the inductive hypothesis each of a and b can be written as a product of primes, from which it follows that $k+1$ can also be written as a product of primes. We now prove that this product is unique. Suppose that $k+1$ has the two prime factorisations

$$p_1 p_2 \cdots p_r \quad \text{and} \quad q_1 q_2 \cdots q_s,$$

for some $r, s \geq 2$. As $p_1 p_2 \cdots p_r = q_1 q_2 \cdots q_s$ and p_1 is prime, it must be the case that $p_1 \mid q_j$ for some j with $1 \leq j \leq s$. In fact $p_1 = q_j$ since p_1 and q_j are both primes. After cancelling these from the prime factorisations of $m+1$ and relabelling the primes q_i if necessary, we obtain

$$p_2 \cdots p_r = q_2 \cdots q_s.$$

Note that $p_2 \cdots p_r < k+1$ since $p_1 \geq 2$. Thus, by the inductive hypothesis, it is the case that the prime decompositions $p_2 \cdots p_r$ and $q_2 \cdots q_s$ are identical (apart from possibly the order of the factors), thereby completing the inductive step and the proof of the theorem. □

It is important to note that in the proof of theorem 2.1 there is no implication that the primes $p_1, p_2, \ldots, p_r$ are distinct. Suppose that there are $m \leq r$ distinct primes in this sequence. Then, on renumbering the subscripts if necessary, theorem 2.1 has the following corollary. A corollary, by the way, is a result that follows easily from a preceding theorem.

Corollary 2.2 *For any $n \geq 2$, there exists a positive integer m such that n may be written in the form*

$$n = p_1^{a_1} p_2^{a_2} \cdots p_m^{a_m},$$

for some unique strictly increasing sequence $p_1, p_2, \ldots, p_m$ of primes and sequence $a_1, a_2, \ldots, a_m$ of positive integers.

Definition 2.3 *Let d, m and n be positive integers, written $d, m, n \in \mathbb{N}$, where d is a common factor of m and n. Then the largest possible value of d is known as the* greatest common divisor *or* highest common factor *of m and n. This is denoted by $d = \gcd(m, n)$.*

Challenge 2.1 Let $m, n \in \mathbb{N}$. Use the prime factorisations of m and n to obtain:

(a) a formula for $\gcd(m, n)$;
(b) a formula for $\operatorname{lcm}(m, n)$, the lowest common multiple of m and n;
(c) a proof that $\gcd(m, n) \times \operatorname{lcm}(m, n) = mn$;
(d) a formula for the number of common factors of m and n;
(e) an efficient method for listing all the common factors of m and n.

Despite the fact that it is a relatively straightforward result, the Fundamental Theorem of Arithmetic lies at the heart of many number-theoretic results. Although the role that it is playing may not always be mentioned explicitly, you will find it cropping up frequently throughout this book.

Exercise 2

1. Obtain the prime factorisations of each of the following:
   (a) $10\,000$;
   (b) $99\,176$;
   (c) 75^9;
   (d) $21!$.

2. Let p be a prime and $m, n \in \mathbb{N}$. If $p \mid m^n$ does it follow that $p^n \mid m^n$? Justify your answer.

3. Let $n \in \mathbb{N}$. Show that:
   (a) $n^2 - 1$ is composite when $n \geq 3$.
   (b) 7 is the only prime number of the form $n^3 - 1$.

4. Let $p(n)$ represent the product of the first n primes. For example, $p(3) = 2 \times 3 \times 5 = 30$. Is it true that $p(n) + 1$ is prime for all $n \in \mathbb{N}$? Investigate.

5. Suppose that $\gcd(m, n) = p$ for some prime p. What possible values could $\gcd(m^4, n^3)$ take?

Chapter 2: The Fundamental Theorem of Arithmetic

6. Use your results from challenge 2.1 to obtain, for 7875 and 5292:
   (a) The highest common factor.
   (b) The lowest common multiple.
   (c) The number of common factors.

7. (a) Find a quick way to calculate the power of 3 in the prime factorisation of 100!.
   (b) Generalise your method from part (a) to enable you to obtain the power of the prime p in the prime factorisation of $n!$.

8. For $n \geq 5$, $n!$ has a number of zeros on the end. For example, as you should check, 12! has two zeros on the end. Figure out an efficient way of working out the number of zeros on the end of $n!$ for any given $n \in \mathbb{N}$.

9. Let p and q be primes satisfying $p \geq q \geq 5$. Prove that $24 \mid (p^2 - q^2)$.

10. Is it true that if $2^n - 1$ is prime then n has to be prime? Explore.

11. Prove that, for $n \geq 3$, a prime can always be found lying strictly between n and $n!$.

12. Given the prime factorisation of $n \in \mathbb{N}$, find a quick way of calculating the number of squares that divide n.

Chapter 3

Summing the reciprocals of the primes

In this chapter we consider some slightly more challenging mathematics, and present a beautiful proof of the fact, referred to in chapter 1, that the sum of the reciprocals of the primes diverges to infinity. What then do mathematicians mean exactly by the phrase 'a beautiful proof'? To my mind, a proof possesses a certain aesthetic quality when there is an elegant simplicity to it, when ideas are combined in novel ways and when the mathematical structure behind it gradually reveals itself.

This theorem might in some sense be regarded as lying somewhere in the vast chasm between Euclid's result on the infinitude of the primes and Dirichlet's theorem. The concepts of convergent and divergent sequences will be needed; see [7] or appendix A if these are unfamiliar to you.

We first look at the behaviour of some rather more well-known series. Let us start with the finite series

$$H_n = \sum_{k=1}^{n} \frac{1}{k},$$

which is called the nth *harmonic number*. For example,

$$H_5 = 1 + \frac{1}{2} + \frac{1}{3} + \frac{1}{4} + \frac{1}{5}$$
$$= \frac{137}{60}.$$

What can be said about H_n as $n \to \infty$? This may not be immediately apparent. However, it can be shown that the *harmonic series* diverges, as follows. For any $k \in \mathbb{N}$ it is the case that

$$H_{2^{k+1}} = H_{2^k} + \frac{1}{2^k+1} + \frac{1}{2^k+2} + \cdots + \frac{1}{2^{k+1}}$$

$$> H_{2^k} + \frac{1}{2^{k+1}} + \frac{1}{2^{k+1}} + \cdots + \frac{1}{2^{k+1}}$$

$$= H_{2^k} + \frac{1}{2},$$

on noting that in the first two lines there are 2^k terms after the term H_{2^k}. From this it follows that

$$H_{2^m} = (H_{2^m} - H_{2^{m-1}}) + (H_{2^{m-1}} - H_{2^{m-2}}) + \cdots + (H_2 - H_1) + H_1 > \frac{m}{2} + 1$$

for any $m \in \mathbb{N}$, which does indeed show that the harmonic series diverges since we can make the sum as large as we like by choosing a suitable value of m.

This means that although some subseries of the harmonic series may converge, others will diverge. The well-known subseries given by

$$\sum_{k=1}^{\infty} \frac{1}{2^k} \quad \text{and} \quad \sum_{k=1}^{\infty} \frac{1}{k^2}$$

both converge. The one on the left is an infinite geometric series with sum 1, and we already know from chapter 1 that the sum of the series on the right is $\frac{\pi^2}{6}$. It is now shown, however, that the subseries comprising the reciprocals of the primes does indeed diverge.

Theorem 3.1

$$\sum_{k=1}^{n} \frac{1}{p_k} \to \infty \quad \text{as} \quad n \to \infty,$$

where p_k is the kth prime.

PROOF It is worth first considering what the statement of this theorem actually means. Consider the sequence $\{s_n\}$, where

$$s_n = \sum_{k=1}^{n} \frac{1}{p_k}.$$

Chapter 3: Summing the reciprocals of the primes

Note that $\{s_n\}$ is a strictly increasing sequence. The theorem states essentially that, for any given $a \in \mathbb{R}$, there exists some $N \in \mathbb{N}$ such that $s_n > a$ for all $n > N$. Putting things a little less formally, for any real number you give me, I will, by summing a sufficiently large number of the prime reciprocals, be able to exceed your number.

Let us fix $N \in \mathbb{N}$. Then there exists some $k \in \mathbb{N}$ such that $N \leq 2^k$. Furthermore, if p_n denotes the nth prime (so that $p_1 = 2$, $p_2 = 3$, and so on) then there exists some $m \in \mathbb{N}$ such that $p_m \leq N < p_{m+1}$; in other words p_m is the largest prime not exceeding N.

Since $N \leq 2^k$, then it must be the case that $N \leq p_i^k$ for $1 \leq i \leq m$. It follows from this that

$$1 + \frac{1}{2} + \cdots + \frac{1}{N} \leq \left(1 + \frac{1}{p_1} + \cdots + \frac{1}{p_1^k}\right)\left(1 + \frac{1}{p_2} + \cdots + \frac{1}{p_2^k}\right)$$
$$\cdots \left(1 + \frac{1}{p_m} + \cdots + \frac{1}{p_m^k}\right).$$

The above inequality may not appear at all obvious initially, but I claim that the right-hand side, when multiplied out, contains every single term on the left-hand side, and many more besides. This is because the denominators of the terms on the right will be each be of the form

$$p_1^{a_1} p_2^{a_2} \cdots p_m^{a_m},$$

where $0 \leq a_i \leq k$ for $1 \leq i \leq m$, and every integer of this form does indeed appear. From the choice of k and the definition of m, therefore, it is the case that every integer from 1 to N inclusive appears as a denominator on the right-hand side (after expanding).

Now note that

$$1 + \frac{1}{p_i} + \cdots + \frac{1}{p_i^k}$$

gives the first $k+1$ terms of the infinite geometric progression

$$\sum_{j=0}^{\infty} \frac{1}{p_i^j}.$$

Therefore, on using the formula for the sum to infinity of a geometric progression, we have

$$1 + \frac{1}{p_i} + \cdots + \frac{1}{p_i^k} < \frac{1}{1 - p_i^{-1}}$$
$$= 1 + \frac{1}{p_i - 1},$$

and hence

$$1 + \frac{1}{2} + \cdots + \frac{1}{N} < \left(1 + \frac{1}{p_1 - 1}\right)\left(1 + \frac{1}{p_2 - 1}\right) \cdots \left(1 + \frac{1}{p_m - 1}\right). \quad (3.1)$$

Next we use the result that $1 + x < e^x$ for any $x \in \mathbb{R}$ such that $x \neq 0$ (see challenge 3.1). Using it in conjunction with result (3.1) leads to

$$1 + \frac{1}{2} + \cdots + \frac{1}{N} < \exp\left(\frac{1}{p_1 - 1}\right) \exp\left(\frac{1}{p_2 - 1}\right) \cdots \exp\left(\frac{1}{p_m - 1}\right)$$
$$< \exp\left(\frac{2}{p_1}\right) \exp\left(\frac{2}{p_2}\right) \cdots \exp\left(\frac{2}{p_m}\right)$$
$$= \exp\left(2\left\{\frac{1}{p_1} + \frac{1}{p_2} + \cdots + \frac{1}{p_m}\right\}\right),$$

where the second line above is true since

$$\frac{1}{p_i - 1} \leq \frac{1}{p_i - \frac{p_i}{2}}$$
$$= \frac{2}{p_i}.$$

Thus

$$\frac{1}{p_1} + \frac{1}{p_2} + \cdots + \frac{1}{p_m} > \frac{1}{2} \log\left(1 + \frac{1}{2} + \cdots + \frac{1}{N}\right).$$

However, we already know that the harmonic series diverges. Therefore, since $\log x \to \infty$ as $x \to \infty$, it follows that the sum of the reciprocals of the primes diverges to infinity. □

Challenge 3.1 Prove that $1 + x < e^x$ for any $x \in \mathbb{R}$ such that $x \neq 0$.

Chapter 3: Summing the reciprocals of the primes

It is worth noting here that

$$\sum_{k=1}^{n} \frac{1}{p_k}$$

grows incredibly slowly as n increases. In order to illustrate this, I used *Mathematica*® to calculate

$$\sum_{k=1}^{50\,000} \frac{1}{p_k} \approx 2.8512 \quad \text{and} \quad \sum_{k=1}^{100\,000} \frac{1}{p_k} \approx 2.9061.$$

Research activity 3.1 Do some investigating to see if you can find a function of n that gives a reasonably good approximation to

$$\sum_{k=1}^{n} \frac{1}{p_k}.$$

Exercise 3

1. Show that the series

$$\frac{1}{7} + \frac{1}{10} + \frac{1}{13} + \frac{1}{16} + \cdots$$

diverges.

2. (a) With H_n denoting the nth harmonic number, prove that

$$H_n = \int_0^1 \frac{1 - x^n}{1 - x} \, dx.$$

  (b) By substituting $u = 1 - x$ into this integral, or otherwise, show that

$$H_n = \sum_{k=1}^{n} \frac{(-1)^{k-1}}{k} \binom{n}{k}.$$

3. Consider

$$\sum_{n \in S} \frac{1}{n},$$

where S is the set of positive integers without a 9 in their decimal representation. Does this sum converge?

4. Explain why

$$\sum_{k=1}^{\infty} \frac{1}{k^2} = \prod_{p} \left(1 - \frac{1}{p^2}\right)^{-1},$$

where the product on the right is over all primes p. Why does result (1.1) then imply that there are infinitely many prime numbers?

Part II

The toolkit

Chapter 4

Arithmetic functions

It is likely that most of the functions you have met thus far in your mathematical studies have been ones like $f(x) = x^2 - 3x$ or $g(x) = \sin 2x$ that are defined for all $x \in \mathbb{R}$, or at least over certain intervals of $\mathbb{R}$. By way of a contrast, in this chapter we encounter a whole class of functions for which the domain is restricted just to the positive integers $\mathbb{N}$. These are called *arithmetic functions*. Not only are their domains different from the functions given above, but the ways in which they are defined tend to be different also. At first sight, their definitions might seem a little more complicated than the sort of symbolic definitions we are used to; some of them even involve conditional statements. A serious study of the additive and multiplicative properties of integers would be virtually impossible without a detailed knowledge of the common arithmetic functions. It is also worth mentioning here that the range of a particular arithmetic function might include integers, numbers or even complex numbers (as we shall see later).

Since Dirichlet's theorem concerns a particular property of the integers, it should not be too surprising that arithmetic functions are going to play a large part in our quest for a proof. Indeed, we will meet a fair number of these functions on our journey, several of which you may find rather esoteric initially. There is a whole body of theory associated with arithmetic functions, and, along with the relevant functions, a number of these ideas and results will be introduced at appropriate points in the book. In this chapter we shall, in order to illustrate some key introductory concepts, look at several well-known arithmetic functions, one of which will actually be utilised in our proof of Dirichlet's theorem.

It is sensible first to consider a nice simple arithmetic function. Let $\tau(n)$ be the *number of factors* of $n \in \mathbb{N}$. Note that the domain of τ is $\mathbb{N}$. For example, the factors of 9 are 1, 3 and 9, while those of 10 are 1, 2, 5 and 10, giving $\tau(9) = 3$ and $\tau(10) = 4$. The graph of this function can be seen in figure 4.1, noting that it consists of a series of dots at the positive integers. It is clear that for small values of n it is very easy to obtain $\tau(n)$ by listing all of the factors. For large n however, this method for finding $\tau(n)$ could become both tedious and error-prone. Is it therefore possible to find some sort of formula that would allow us to calculate $\tau(n)$ without having to go through the laborious process of having to list all the factors? It turns out that there is in fact a formula, but it is not in terms of n directly.

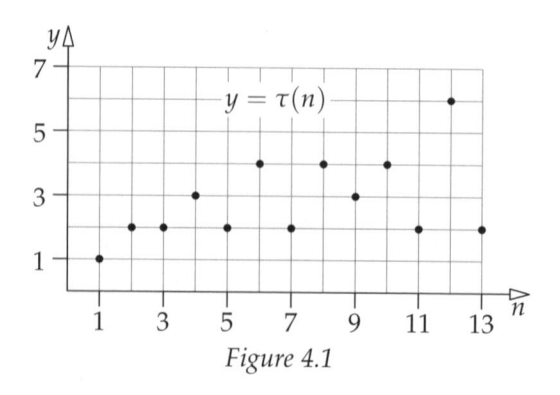

Figure 4.1

Recall that for any $n \geq 2$ the Fundamental Theorem of Arithmetic tells us that n can be written as

$$n = p_1^{a_1} p_2^{a_2} \cdots p_m^{a_m},$$

for some unique strictly increasing sequence $p_1, p_2, \ldots, p_m$ of primes and sequence $a_1, a_2, \ldots, a_m$ of positive integers; see corollary 2.2. Suppose that d is a factor of n. Then it must be the case that

$$d = p_1^{b_1} p_2^{b_2} \cdots p_m^{b_m},$$

where $0 \leq b_k \leq a_k$, $k = 1, 2, 3, \ldots, m$. If $n = 2^5 \times 7 \times 11^2 \times 17^2 \times 31 = 242\,824\,736$, for example, then $d = 2^2 \times 7^0 \times 11^2 \times 17 \times 31 = 255\,068$ is a factor of n.

Note that for any factor d there are $a_1 + 1$ ways of choosing the exponent of p_1 since $0 \leq b_1 \leq a_1$. Similarly there are $a_2 + 1$ ways of choosing

Chapter 4: Arithmetic functions

the exponent of p_2, and so on. By the Fundamental Theorem of Arithmetic, distinct sequences of exponents give rise to distinct factors of n. Therefore, since the number of factors of n is equal to the total number of ways in which these exponents may be chosen, it follows that

$$\tau(n) = (a_1 + 1)(a_2 + 1) \cdots (a_m + 1).$$

The number of factors of 242 824 736 is thus $(5+1)(1+1)(2+1)(2+1)(1+1) = 216$.

Before moving on, it is worth considering some of the simple properties of $\tau(n)$ in order to appreciate how such functions encode properties of n. For example, $\tau(n) = 2$ if, and only if, n is prime. And $\tau(n)$ is odd precisely when all of $a_1 + 1, a_2 + 1, \ldots, a_m + 1$ are all odd, which occurs when all of $a_1, a_2, \ldots, a_m$ are even. Thus $\tau(n)$ is odd if, and only if, n is a square number.

Challenge 4.1 Let $\sigma(n)$ be the *sum of the factors* of n. For example, the factors of 10 are 1, 2, 5 and 10, so that $\sigma(10) = 1 + 2 + 5 + 10 = 18$. As for $\tau(n)$, it is very easy to calculate $\sigma(n)$ for small values of n by listing factors; although in the present case this list needs to be summed rather than simply counted. For large n however, this method becomes very tedious once again. The aim of this challenge is to find a way of calculating $\sigma(n)$ from its prime factorisation. Here are some ideas to get you started, but try to use your own initiative as much as possible:

(a) What is $\sigma(n)$ when n is a prime number?
(b) What is $\sigma(n)$ when $n = p^k$ is a power of a prime?
(c) Can you use the formula for the sum of a finite geometric series to simplify your previous answer?
(d) Say that $n = pq$, where p and q are distinct primes. What is $\sigma(n)$ in this case? Will your expression factorise?
(e) How about if $n = p^a q^b$ with p and q distinct primes and $a, b \in \mathbb{N}$? Use the above results to give a simplified expression for $\sigma(n)$.
(f) Now obtain a general result, and then try out a few numerical examples to verify that your formula seems to be working.

Notice the inextricable connection between the calculation of τ and the Fundamental Theorem of Arithmetic, and similarly for σ. On looking at further arithmetic functions, you will notice that this is a common theme.

Let us now briefly consider a useful property possessed by many of the common arithmetic functions. Take τ, for example. We have $\tau(5) = 2$, $\tau(6) = 4$ and $\tau(30) = 8$, showing that

$$\tau(5 \times 6) = \tau(30) = \tau(5)\tau(6).$$

Similarly, $\tau(12) = 6$, $\tau(25) = 3$ and $\tau(300) = 18$, showing that

$$\tau(12 \times 25) = \tau(300) = \tau(12)\tau(25).$$

Of course, on the basis of such slim evidence, it might be unwise to conjecture that $\tau(mn) = mn$ for all positive integers m and n. Indeed, since $\tau(4) = 3$, $\tau(10) = 4$ and $\tau(40) = 8 \neq 12$, it can be seen that this conjecture is false. However, all is not lost since it does turn out to be true that

$$\tau(mn) = \tau(m)\tau(n) \quad \text{whenever} \quad \gcd(m,n) = 1.$$

It is actually a fairly simple matter to show that this is the case, for if $\gcd(m,n) = 1$ then it is possible to write

$$m = p_1^{a_1} p_2^{a_2} \cdots p_i^{a_i} \quad \text{and} \quad n = q_1^{b_1} q_2^{b_2} \cdots q_j^{b_j},$$

where these two factorisations have no primes in common. Therefore,

$$\begin{aligned}\tau(mn) &= \tau\left(p_1^{a_1} p_2^{a_2} \cdots p_i^{a_i} q_1^{b_1} q_2^{b_2} \cdots q_j^{b_j}\right) \\ &= (a_1 + 1)(a_2 + 1) \cdots (a_i + 1)(b_1 + 1)(b_2 + 1) \cdots (b_j + 1) \\ &= \tau(m)\tau(n).\end{aligned}$$

Definition 4.1 *An arithmetic function f for which $f(mn) = f(m)f(n)$ whenever $\gcd(m,n) = 1$ is called a* multiplicative function.

Thus τ, for example, is a multiplicative function, and challenge 4.1 shows that σ is also multiplicative. The reason why this is a particularly useful property for an arithmetic function to have is that, since $\gcd(p^a, q^b) = 1$ for any positive integers a and b, and distinct primes p and q, the function τ will be completely determined once its values at the prime powers are known.

Any arithmetic function f that does happen to possess the property that $f(mn) = f(m)f(n)$ for all positive integers m and n is called *completely multiplicative*. A simple example of such a function is given by $f(n) = n^k$ for some fixed number k.

Chapter 4: Arithmetic functions

Challenge 4.2 Let $f(n)$ be a multiplicative arithmetic function. Prove that either $f(1) = 1$ or $f(n) = 0$ for all positive integers n.

We now come to an arithmetic function that, as will be seen, plays a prominent role in the proof of Dirichlet's theorem. It is named after the Swiss mathematician Leonhard Euler (1707–1783) mentioned in chapter 1; one of the greatest mathematicians that has ever lived.

Definition 4.2 *The arithmetic function $\phi(n)$, known as* Euler's phi-function *or the* Euler totient function, *is defined to be the number of positive integers, up to and including n, that are coprime to n.*

In other words, $\phi(n)$ counts the number of integers m with the property that $m \in \{1, 2, 3, \ldots, n\}$ and $\gcd(m, n) = 1$. For example, 1, 2, 4, 5, 7 and 8 are all coprime to 9, whereas 3, 6 and 9 are not, so that $\phi(9) = 6$.

Challenge 4.3 It is well worth spending some time getting to know Euler's phi-function:

(a) Investigate $\phi(n)$, with the ultimate aim of obtaining a method for calculating it without having to list all of the numbers up to and including n that are coprime to n. It might be a good idea to start by just considering the situation where n is a power of a prime; in other words when $n = p^k$ for some prime p and positive integer k. See if you can find a formula for $\phi(n)$ in terms of p and k, explaining why it works. You might then be able to generalise your result to cover any n.

(b) Show that $\phi(n)$ is a multiplicative function. If you managed to obtain a general formula in part (a) then the fact that $\phi(n)$ is multiplicative follows from this. On the other hand, it is possible (but not entirely straightforward) to show that $\phi(n)$ is multiplicative without using a formula.

Finally, let us return to the notion of the domain of a function. The graph of $f(x) = 2\sqrt{x}$, with natural domain $x \geq 0$, is shown in figure 4.2. Note that this domain may be restricted to, for example, the positive integers. The graph of the resultant function appears in figure 4.3.

A question we may now ask ourselves is as follows: Is it possible to go the other way? In other words, can we extend the domain of an arithmetic

Figure 4.2

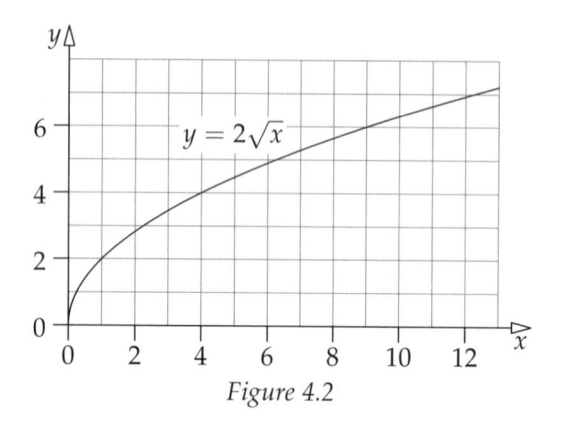

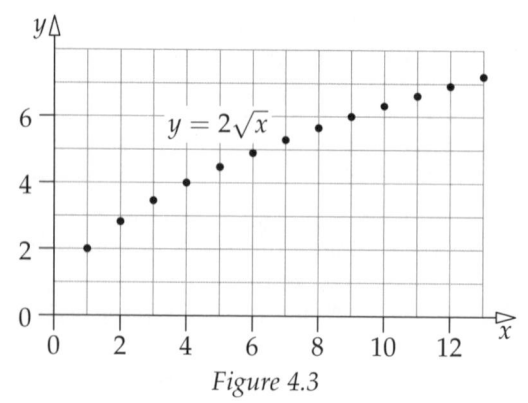

Figure 4.3

function to the positive reals or even to $\mathbb{R}$? It turns out, in most cases at least, that this would simply not make sense. After all, the definitions of these functions tend to be based on specific properties of the positive integers. How, for example, might $\tau(\sqrt{10})$ be interpreted?

It is possible, however, to define a function of x, having domain $x > 0$, in terms of the sum of the values of an arithmetic function for all $n \leq x$. For example, with
$$f(x) = \sum_{n \leq x} \tau(n),$$
then
$$f(\sqrt{10}) = \sum_{n \leq \sqrt{10}} \tau(n)$$
$$= \tau(1) + \tau(2) + \tau(3)$$

$$= 1 + 2 + 2$$
$$= 5.$$

Admittedly, the above example might well seem a little contrived; indeed, it will be of no use to us whatsoever. However, functions of these types can sometimes provide more useful information. For example, let

$$f(n) = \begin{cases} 1 & \text{if } n \text{ is prime} \\ 0 & \text{otherwise.} \end{cases}$$

Then it may be seen that the function F given by

$$F(x) = \sum_{n \leq x} f(n)$$

evaluates the number of primes no larger than x. In fact, this function has been the subject of so much study over the last two centuries that it even has its own symbol, $\pi(x)$; it ought to be noted that this has nothing to do with the number π. The function $\pi(x)$ 'jumps' at each prime and then stays constant until the next one. It is thus known as a *step function*, as is clear on considering figure 4.4. The blobs indicate what happens at the extreme ends of each horizontal step. For example, the filled-in and empty blobs at $(5,3)$ and $(5,2)$ respectively, tell us that $\pi(5) = 3$ rather than $\pi(5) = 2$.

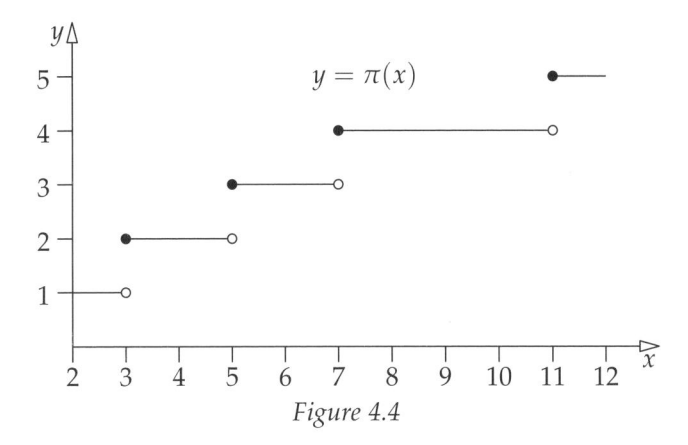

Figure 4.4

Of course, if we wanted to know how many primes there were below 10^{20} then this function, as its definition stands, is probably not going to be of much use. It would be necessary to obtain either some relatively simple expression for $\pi(x)$ in terms of x, or at the very least, an expression that gives an approximate formula for $\pi(x)$. This is indeed the territory of the Prime Number Theorem, which is another of the truly great theorems in mathematics; see chapter 19 for further details.

Note that $\pi(x)$ may be regarded as a 'counting' function. Our aims here are rather less lofty than those of the Prime Number Theorem since we do not actually require a formula giving the number of primes appearing up to some specified point in a particular arithmetic progression; rather, we simply want to know whether or not the number of primes in this progression tends to infinity as x does. As will eventually be seen in chapters 14 and 15, this is achieved by finding and then analysing an expression, in the form of a sum, that tends to infinity if, and only if, the number of primes in the arithmetic progression tends to infinity.

Exercise 4

1. Using the formula for $\tau(n)$ in terms of the prime factorisation of n, calculate the number of factors of
   (a) $1\,000\,000$
   (b) 7455
   (c) 24^2
   (d) $8!$.

2. Now use the formula for $\tau(n)$ to list all n having exactly six factors for $n \leq 50$.

3. What is the smallest positive integer n for which
   (a) $\tau(n) = \tau(n+1)$
   (b) $\tau(n) = \tau(n+1) = \tau(n+2)$?

4. (a) Evaluate $\pi(50)$ and $\pi(\sqrt{50})$.
   (b) Find all positive integers m satisfying $\pi(m+5) - \pi(m) = 3$. Explain your answer.
   (c) Let p be an odd prime. If $p+2$ is also a prime then p and $p+2$ are called a pair of *twin primes*. Find all pairs of twin primes below 100. Many mathematicians believe that are in fact

infinitely many pairs of twin primes; this is the famous twin prime conjecture (see [4], for example).

5. Prove each of the following:
   (a) $\phi(3n) = 3\phi(n)$ if, and only if, 3 is a factor of n.
   (b) If $\phi(n) \mid (n-1)$ then the exponent of each prime appearing in the prime factorisation of n is 1.

6. Show that $\sigma(n)$ is odd if, and only if, n is either a square number or double a square number.

7. (a) Find a number n such that $\sigma(n) = 2n$.
   (b) Any n with the property given in part (a) is called a *perfect number*. Show that $n = 2^{k-1}(2^k - 1)$ is perfect if $2^k - 1$ is prime.

Chapter 5

Limits and 'big oh' notation

Dirichlet's theorem concerns a property of the integers, but its proof requires us to analyse certain functions defined on the positive real numbers. The nature of these functions means that it will be necessary to utilise something called 'big oh' notation, so called because of the symbol used! If $g(x)$ is some specified function of x then $O(g(x))$ represents an unspecified function of x which grows no faster than some constant multiplied by $g(x)$. That probably was not particularly enlightening, so I will introduce 'big oh' by way of an example.

Consider the function $h(x) = f(x) + g(x)$ where, for $x > 0$,

$$f(x) = x^3 + 5x^2 \quad \text{and} \quad g(x) = \frac{7x^2 \sin x}{x+3}.$$

Suppose that we wanted to know whether or not

$$h(x) \to \infty \quad \text{as} \quad x \to \infty.$$

Notice that $f(x)$ takes only positive values when $x > 0$ while $g(x)$ takes both positive and negative values. It might not immediately be apparent, therefore, that $h(x) \to \infty$ as $x \to \infty$. However, it is evident that f in some sense 'dominates' g when x is large, and, although g cannot just be thrown away, it might be useful to have a way of expressing its magnitude in terms of the magnitude of a simpler function.

Indeed, by noting that $|\sin x| \leq 1$ for all real x, it may be seen that $|g(x)| \leq 7x$ for all positive real x. In other words, there exists a positive constant M such that $|g(x)| \leq Mx$ for all $x > 0$. We could, for example, choose M to be 7 in this particular case. When g satisfies such a condition we write $g(x) = O(x)$, giving

$$h(x) = x^3 + 5x^2 + O(x).$$

An interpretation of this is that $h(x)$ is $x^3 + 5x^2$ plus some unspecified function, the magnitude of which is never more than some fixed constant multiplied by x.

With h in this form it is clear, from our knowledge of polynomials, that $h(x) \to \infty$ as $x \to \infty$. Of course, in this particular example, it was all rather obvious. In our proof of Dirichlet's theorem, however, we are going to encounter far more complicated functions whose behaviour is more or less impossible to ascertain simply by inspection. Indeed, it will be necessary to make judicious use of 'big oh' notation throughout the rest of this book in order to help analyse the behaviour, as $x \to \infty$, of a number of awkward functions. It provides us with a useful shorthand to get a handle on some really rather difficult summations.

It is possible to go one step further in using the 'big oh' notation on h and write $h(x) = x^3 + O(x^2)$, noting that $O(x^2)$ is able to 'swallow up' both $5x^2$ and $O(x)$. To see that this is the case, note that for some $M > 0$ and all $x \geq M$,

$$|5x^2 + O(x)| \leq 5x^2 + Mx$$
$$\leq 5x^2 + x^2$$
$$= 6x^2.$$

However, in doing so we lose yet more information about h, and how far this process is taken will very much depend on what h is going to be used for. It is also true that $h(x) = O(x^3)$, but then so much information about h will have been lost that it is not now even possible to give its order of magnitude for large x, as could have been done when writing $h(x) = x^3 + 5x^2 + O(x)$ or $h(x) = x^3 + O(x^2)$. Note that it would also be mathematically correct, though totally pointless, to write $h(x) = O(x^4)$. Incidentally, when using 'big oh' it is a convention that the right-hand side of the equation does not give more information than the left-hand side.

Challenge 5.1   Show that

$$(3x - 5)^4 + 15x^2 \log x = 81x^4 + O(x^3).$$

Let us now make things a little more general and fully define the 'big oh' notation.

Definition 5.1 *We write $f(x) = O(g(x))$ to mean that there exist real positive constants M and a, and functions $f(x)$ and $g(x)$ with $g(x) > 0$ for all $x \geq a$, such that $|f(x)| \leq Mg(x)$ for all $x \geq a$.*

Challenge 5.2 Of the following four examples using 'big-oh' notation, three are correct but one is wrong. See if you can identify and correct the error.

(a) $3\cos x + 2 = O(1)$.

(b) $5x^2 \log x + 3x^2 - 4x = O(x^2 \log x)$.

(c) $\dfrac{3x^4 + 2x^2 - 5}{x^2 - 5} + 2x + 1 = O(x^2)$.

(d) $\dfrac{1}{x^2} + \dfrac{2\sin x}{x} = O\left(\dfrac{1}{x^2}\right)$.

We will be meeting functions of the positive real number x, involving sums of arithmetic functions, that may not be possible to express exactly in a simple analytic form. All the same, we would like to have some information regarding their behaviour when x gets large. A simple example of a function of this type is

$$F(x) = \sum_{n \leq x} n,$$

where the sum is to be evaluated over all positive integers no greater than the positive real number x. Although this is not a function that will be used in the proof of Dirichlet's theorem, it does allow us neatly to illustrate some key ideas that will be utilised throughout.

Table 5.1 gives $F(x)$ evaluated at various positive real numbers: It can be seen that $F(x)$ is yet another example of a step function in that its value suddenly jumps up when it reaches an integer and then stays constant until it gets to the next integer; remember that we met a function of this type in chapter 4. It is clear that $F(x)$ cannot be expressed in terms of some simple analytic function. It is possible, however, to use 'big-oh' to say something about its behaviour as x increases. If $x \geq 1$ then we can

x	$F(x)$
1	1
$\sqrt{2}$	1
2	$1+2=3$
$2\frac{1}{5}$	$1+2=3$
3	$1+2+3=6$
π	$1+2+3=6$

Table 5.1

write $x = n + t$ for some $n \in \mathbb{N}$ and $t \in \mathbb{R}$ such that $0 \leq t < 1$. This gives

$$F(x) = \tfrac{1}{2}n(n+1)$$
$$= \tfrac{1}{2}(x-t)(x-t+1)$$
$$= \tfrac{1}{2}x^2 + \left(\tfrac{1}{2} - t\right)x + \tfrac{1}{2}t(t-1).$$

When x gets large, the dominant term is clearly $\tfrac{1}{2}x^2$.

Challenge 5.3   Show that, when $0 \leq t \leq 1$,

$$\left|\left(\tfrac{1}{2} - t\right)x + \tfrac{1}{2}t(t-1)\right| \leq \tfrac{1}{2}x$$

for all $x \geq 1$.

Thus, using the result of challenge 5.3, $F(x)$ can be thought of as $\tfrac{1}{2}x^2$ plus some function whose modulus never exceeds $\tfrac{1}{2}x$. In other words,

$$F(x) = \tfrac{1}{2}x^2 + O(x).$$

When comparing this to the formal definition of 'big oh' you will see that we can put $M = \tfrac{1}{2}$ and $a = 1$ here.

A mathematical statement such as the one above, providing us with information on the behaviour of a function of x as x gets large, is called an *asymptotic relation*. Note that it does not say that $F(x)$ gets closer to $\tfrac{1}{2}x^2$ as x increases; in fact, some quick calculations should convince you that the larger x becomes the further $F(x)$ tends to be from $\tfrac{1}{2}x^2$. What the relation does imply, however, is that the relative error in using $\frac{1}{2}x^2$ for $F(x)$ tends to zero as x tends to infinity. By this we mean that

$$\frac{F(x) - \frac{1}{2}x^2}{F(x)} \to 0 \quad \text{as} \quad x \to \infty.$$

Finally in this chapter, it is worth mentioning an interesting fact about logarithms, as these functions will play a large part in the proof of Dirichlet's theorem. The function

$$f(x) = \log_b x$$

is an increasing function of x for any base $b > 1$ and $\log_b x \to \infty$ as $x \to \infty$. However, these functions increase extremely slowly with x, in the following sense. Suppose that a is a fixed positive real number. Then, for any $b > 1$, there exists some positive real number, X say, such that

$$x^a > \log_b x \text{ for all } x > X,$$
$$\text{so} \quad \log_b x = O(x^a) \text{ for all } a > 0.$$

Even if $a = 10^{-30}$, for example, then for any given $b > 1$ it would still be possible to find a number X such that x^a eventually overtakes $\log_b x$ and stays ahead of it for all $x > X$. Of course, X might have to be very large indeed, but the key thing is that there does exist such a value of x.

Knowledge of the algebraic properties of 'big oh' will be assumed as a matter of course in many of the calculations throughout the rest of this book. At times it will be necessary to simplify reasonably complicated expressions involving 'big oh'. It is therefore particularly important that full attempts are made at all of the questions in the following exercise.

Research activity 5.1 There is also a 'little oh' notation. See what you can find out about it.

Exercise 5

1. Let $f(x) = 3x^3 - 2\log x$ and $g(x) = 3x^2 - 5x$. Express each of the following in the form $ax^b + O(h(x))$ for some $a, b \in \mathbb{N}$ and

function $h(x)$:
(a) $f(x) + 5g(x)$;
(b) $f(x) - g(x)$;
(c) $f(x) - xg(x)$;
(d) $\dfrac{f(x)}{g(x)}$.

2. Prove and then generalise each of the following:
   (a) $O(x^2) + O(x^2) = O(x^2)$.
   (b) $O(O(\sqrt{x})) = O(\sqrt{x})$.
   (c) $O\left(\dfrac{2x-3}{\log x}\right) = (2x-3)O\left(\dfrac{1}{\log x}\right)$.

3. Let $F(x)$ be defined by
$$F(x) = \sum_{n \leq x} 12(n+5)^2.$$

Express $F(x)$ in the form $ax^b + O(x^c)$, where $a, b, c \in \mathbb{N}$ are to be found.

4. Explain what is wrong with the following argument:

"Since $n = O(n)$, $2n = O(n)$, and so on, then
$$\sum_{k=1}^{n} kn = \sum_{k=1}^{n} O(n) = O(n^2)."$$

5. Prove that, as stated in the text, if a is a fixed positive real number, then, for any $b > 1$, there exists some positive real number X such that $x^a > \log_b x$ for all $x > X$.
   This might be carried out using the following steps:
   (a) By putting $t = x^a$ and changing from base b to base e, explain why it suffices to prove that $\dfrac{\log t}{t} \to 0$ as $t \to \infty$.
   (b) Use the result of challenge 3.1 to show that $\sqrt{t} > \tfrac{1}{2}\log t$ and hence the result in (a).

6. Show that $x\left(\sqrt[x]{x} - 1\right)$ behaves like $\log x$ for large x by obtaining the result
$$x\left(\sqrt[x]{x} - 1\right) = \log x + O\left(\frac{(\log x)^2}{x}\right).$$

Chapter 6

Groups

The theory of groups is an abstract yet fascinating area of mathematics, primarily concerned with algebraic structure. In order to make further progress in our quest to prove Dirichlet's theorem we will, in chapter 9, need to introduce some special arithmetic functions called Dirichlet characters. These functions have some nice properties that can be utilised to derive useful results regarding the primes appearing in any given arithmetic progression. In particular, they may be used to obtain certain amenable sums over just the primes appearing in an arithmetic progression, but more on this later.

The reason that it is necessary to bring in group theory here is that the structural properties of Dirichlet characters can best be described in group-theoretical terms. In order to gain some initial insight into the concept of what a group actually is, it is best first to consider a 'concrete' example.

We will start by looking at $\mathbb{Z}$, the set of integers. On choosing any two numbers, a and b say, from $\mathbb{Z}$ then their sum $a + b$ will also be in $\mathbb{Z}$. For example, $-3, 11 \in \mathbb{Z}$ and $-3 + 11 = 8 \in \mathbb{Z}$. Also, if c is any other element of $\mathbb{Z}$ then $(a + b) + c = a + (b + c)$. These are two properties of numbers that we take very much for granted. The first is called the *closure* of $\mathbb{Z}$ with respect to multiplication and the second the *associativity* of addition in $\mathbb{Z}$.

Let us seek some more 'obvious' properties of the elements from $\mathbb{Z}$. Another one is that there exists a number $e \in \mathbb{Z}$ such that $e + a = a + e = a$ for any choice of $a \in \mathbb{Z}$. Of course e is the number 0; we call this the *identity* with respect to addition in $\mathbb{Z}$. Note that 0 is the only element in $\mathbb{Z}$ that satisfies this condition. Also, for any $a \in \mathbb{Z}$ there exists an element $d \in \mathbb{Z}$ such that $a + d = d + a = 0$. The element $d = -a$ is called the *inverse* of a with respect to addition in $\mathbb{Z}$, and it is clear that each element of $\mathbb{Z}$ has a unique inverse in $\mathbb{Z}$.

The above properties may be summarised as follows:

Closure If a and b are in $\mathbb{Z}$ then so is $a + b$.
Associativity For any $a, b, c \in \mathbb{Z}$ it is true that $(a + b) + c = a + (b + c)$.
Existence of identity The element $0 \in \mathbb{Z}$ is such that $0 + a = a + 0 = a$ for any $a \in \mathbb{Z}$.
Existence of inverses For any $a \in \mathbb{Z}$ we have $a + d = d + a = 0$ where $d = -a$.

Any non-empty set G equipped with a binary operation for which the above four properties (axioms) are satisfied is called a *group*. By a 'binary operation' we mean a mapping from $G \times G$ to G; just think of it as a rule that gives us a way of combining any two elements from G to produce another element from G. It is important to note that a set of elements G cannot, on its own, comprise a group. It is necessary also to specify a binary operation on the elements of G. We say that G is a group *with respect to* this binary operation.

We have already seen that the set of integers is a group with respect to the binary operation consisting of addition; in shorthand this may be written as $(\mathbb{Z}, +)$. Let us try to find another example of a group. Is it true that the set of real numbers $\mathbb{R}$ is a group with respect to multiplication? Any two real numbers multiplied together give another real number, so closure is certainly satisfied. Multiplication of real numbers is also associative. Since $1 \times a = a \times 1 = a$ for any $a \in \mathbb{R}$, then 1 is an identity. We just now need to check the last property. Does every real number possess a multiplicative inverse? In other words, given any $a \in \mathbb{R}$, does there exist $b \in \mathbb{R}$ such that $ab = ba = 1$? The element a does in fact have the inverse $\frac{1}{a}$ unless $a = 0$. This single exception, however, means that not all the elements of $\mathbb{R}$ have multiplicative inverses, so the last condition is not satisfied. Therefore, $\mathbb{R}$ is not a group with respect to multiplication. However, as you should check, if we remove 0 from $\mathbb{R}$ then what remains, written as $\mathbb{R}\backslash\{0\}$, *is* a group with respect to multiplication, a fact that is denoted by $(\mathbb{R}\backslash\{0\}, \times)$.

Challenge 6.1 Show that the set of rational numbers $\mathbb{Q}$ is a group with respect to addition. Is $\mathbb{Q}$ a group with respect to multiplication?

It is quite possible at this point that you might be saying "So what?". After all, these are properties of numbers that you will have been using, and probably taking for granted, for many years now. Well, the truly fascinating thing is that the structural properties listed above occur in a range of different mathematical situations, many of which might initially appear unrelated. They can be found when studying the multiplication of non-zero real numbers, addition of rationals, addition and multiplication of matrices, products of permutations, the composition of functions, and so on. Indeed, it turns out that the study of general sets of elements endowed with such a structure leads to some deep mathematics. It will barely be possible to scratch the surface in this chapter, although we do cover sufficient detail for our immediate needs.

Definition 6.1 *If $a, b \in G$ then ab is used to denote the product of these two elements. This is known as* multiplicative notation. *It is important to appreciate that, although we shall mainly be concerned in this book with multiplication of numbers, this notation can be used to represent other binary operations. A further point with respect to this notation is that a^n is used to represent the product $aaa \cdots a$, where there are n consecutive as. Finally, a^{-1} denotes the multiplicative inverse of a, and we write $\left(a^{-1}\right)^n$ as a^{-n}.*

A subtle consequence of associativity is that it does not matter how we bracket a product such as $aaa \cdots a$ in order to evaluate it. For example, we can omit brackets in the arguments below.

We are now in a position to be able to derive some straightforward results concerning the elements of a group. Let a and b be two elements of the group G with identity e. Then, from the definition of the inverse of an element,

$$abb^{-1}a^{-1} = aea^{-1}$$
$$= aa^{-1}$$
$$= e,$$

which implies that $(ab)^{-1}$, the inverse of ab, is given by $b^{-1}a^{-1}$. Further-

more,
$$(a^{-1}ba)^2 = a^{-1}baa^{-1}ba$$
$$= a^{-1}b^2a,$$
a result which generalises to $(a^{-1}ba)^n = a^{-1}b^na$.

Challenge 6.2 Suppose that G is a group with respect to some binary operation. Establish from the group axioms that G has a unique identity and that the inverse for any $a \in G$ is unique.

Definition 6.2 *If a group G with respect to some binary operation has the property that $ab = ba$ for all $a, b \in G$, then G is called an* abelian group. *In this case the binary operation is termed* commutative.

Although the specific examples of groups we have identified thus far have been abelian, it should not be assumed that this is a general property of groups. Consider, for example, the set of functions

$$e(x) = x \qquad f(x) = 1 - x \qquad g(x) = \frac{1}{x}$$
$$h(x) = \frac{1}{1-x} \qquad i(x) = \frac{x-1}{x} \qquad j(x) = \frac{x}{x-1}$$

where $x \in \mathbb{R}\setminus\{0, 1\}$. It is straightforward to show this set forms a group with respect to composition of functions (where $e(x)$ is the identity). We have

$$f(g(x)) = f\left(\frac{1}{x}\right)$$
$$= 1 - \frac{1}{x}$$
$$= \frac{x-1}{x}$$
$$= i(x),$$

while

$$g(f(x)) = g(1-x)$$
$$= \frac{1}{1-x}$$
$$= h(x).$$

This demonstrates the fact that $fg \neq gf$, so this group is not abelian. In order to prove Dirichlet's theorem, however, we will only be considering groups of numbers (including complex numbers), which are all abelian.

Note that the above group of functions contains finitely many elements, as opposed to the groups considered previously. The number of elements in a finite group is known as the *order* of that group. Our group of functions thus has order 6. Another group with a finite number of elements is $G = \{1, -1\}$ with respect to multiplication. The product of any two elements of G is also in G, we know that ordinary multiplication of numbers is associative, 1 is obviously the identity in this case, and, finally, each element has an inverse in G since $1 \times 1 = 1$ and $(-1) \times (-1) = 1$. Thus G, along with the binary operation of multiplication, is a *finite group*.

This last example brings us nicely on to another concept; that of a *subgroup*. Notice that G satisfies the following:

(a) G is a group when equipped with the same binary operation as the group $(\mathbb{R}\backslash\{0\}, \times)$;
(b) all of the elements of G are contained in $\mathbb{R}\backslash\{0\}$.

When the above is true we say that $(G, \times)$ is a subgroup of $(\mathbb{R}\backslash\{0\}, \times)$. In the above example $(G, \times)$ is a finite subgroup of the infinite group $(\mathbb{R}\backslash\{0\}, \times)$. Note, however, that $(\mathbb{R}\backslash\{0\}, \times)$ also has infinite subgroups such as $(\mathbb{Q}\backslash\{0\}, \times)$, the group consisting of all non-zero rational numbers with respect to multiplication. When considering possible subgroups of a group it is very important to remember (a) above, as the following example illustrates.

Consider the set $T = \{1, 3\}$ along with the binary operation multiplication modulo 4, which means that we take any two numbers from T, multiply them together, and then find the remainder when their product is divided by 4. For example, the product of 3 and 3 is 9, which has remainder 1 when divided by 4. This is written as $3 \times 3 \equiv 1 \pmod 4$; see appendix C if you are not familiar with modular arithmetic. Because also $1 \times 3 \equiv 3 \times 1 \equiv 3 \pmod 4$ and $1 \times 1 \equiv 1 \pmod 4$, T is certainly closed.

You should check the other three requirements to satisfy yourself that T, along with multiplication modulo 4, is in fact a group. This is denoted by $(T, \otimes_4)$. Now T is also contained in $\mathbb{R}\backslash\{0\}$ but is $(T, \otimes_4)$ a subgroup of $(\mathbb{R}\backslash\{0\}, \times)$? I hope you can spot straight away that it is not since the binary operations are not the same. Since $3 \times 3 = 9$, it can be seen that T is not even closed under normal multiplication, the binary operation on $\mathbb{R}\backslash\{0\}$.

Challenge 6.3 Let $G = \{1, 3, 7, 9\}$. Show that G is a group with respect to multiplication modulo 10.

Definition 6.3 Let $k \in \mathbb{N}$ and $S = \{1, 2, 3, \ldots, k\}$. Then $R_k = \{n \in S : \gcd(k, n) = 1\}$ is called the set of reduced residue classes modulo k. Note that R_k has $\phi(k)$ elements, where ϕ is Euler's phi function, as given in definition 4.2.

If $k = 15$, for example, then the set of positive integers that are both less than k and coprime to it is given by $R_{15} = \{1, 2, 4, 7, 8, 11, 13, 14\}$, the set of reduced residue classes modulo 15. It is worth checking that this set is actually closed with respect to multiplication modulo 15. So, for example,

$$7 \times 8 = 56 \equiv 11 \pmod{15} \quad \text{and} \quad 4 \times 13 = 52 \equiv 7 \pmod{15}.$$

You might like to show that R_{15} with respect to multiplication modulo 15 is a group, written $(R_{15}, \otimes_{15})$, and then try finding some subgroups; $\{1, 4, 7, 13\}$ is one of them.

Challenge 6.4 Prove that the set of reduced residue classes modulo k with respect to multiplication modulo k will always be a finite abelian group of order $\phi(k)$, $(R_k, \otimes_k)$. One result from number theory that you might find useful says that if $\gcd(a, k) = 1$ then there exists a unique integer b modulo k such that $ab \equiv 1 \pmod{k}$. If you need a hint then refer to the discussion at the end of appendix C.

For finite groups we can construct what is known as a *group table* (also known as a *Cayley table*). For example, as is easily checked, table 6.1 gives the group table for the group studied in challenge 6.3. Note that table 6.1 has the *Latin square* property in that every element of G appears exactly once in each row and each column. Those familiar with Sudoku puzzles will have encountered this property before. This is the case for any finite group, and you might like to have a go at proving it; see challenge 6.6. The converse is not true, however. In other words, if an $n \times n$ table has the Latin square property then it does necessarily follow that there exists a group with such a table.

Chapter 6: Groups 49

⊗₁₀	1	3	7	9
1	1	3	7	9
3	3	9	1	7
7	7	1	9	3
9	9	7	3	1

Table 6.1

Challenge 6.5 Explain how the group axioms are reflected in the Cayley table of a finite group. Then give an example of a Latin square that cannot be the Cayley table of a finite group.

It is also worth pointing out that table 6.1 is symmetrical about its main diagonal. This is true for all finite abelian groups, so long as the rows and columns are arranged in the same order. In fact, in what follows we will only be dealing with finite abelian groups.

Challenge 6.6 Let $G = \{a_1, a_2, \ldots, a_n\}$ be a finite group, with respect to some binary operation. Show that, for any $a \in G$, $G = \{a_1 a, a_2 a, \ldots, a_n a\}$. This is a generalised version of theorem C.2 on page 162.

In chapter 8 we shall need the following definition associated with the elements of a group.

Definition 6.4 *Let G be a finite group with identity e. The* order $o(a)$ *of an element $a \in G$ is the smallest positive integer n such that, using multiplicative notation, $a^n = e$.*

For example, on considering the group in challenge 6.3,

$$3^2 \equiv 9 \pmod{10},$$
$$3^3 = 27 \equiv 7 \pmod{10},$$
$$3^4 = 81 \equiv 1 \pmod{10},$$

which shows that the element 3 has order 4 in G. This is written as $o(3) = 4$. We now prove some simple results about orders of elements in finite groups.

Theorem 6.5 *Let G be a finite group.*
(a) *For $a \in G$ there is a smallest positive integer n such that $a^n = e$ (so $o(a)$ is well-defined).*
(b) *If $a^m = e$ for some $m \in \mathbb{N}$ then $o(a) \mid m$.*

PROOF Suppose that G had k elements. If $k = 1$ then $a = e$ and we have finished. So assume now that $k \geq 2$. Then by the pigeonhole principle, the list $a, a^2, \ldots, a^{k+1}$ contains a pair of identical elements. In other words, $a^i = a^j$ for some $i, j \in \mathbb{N}$ where, without loss of generality $1 \leq i < j \leq k+1$. On multiplying both sides of this equality by a^{-i} we obtain $a^{j-i} = e$, which shows that there does indeed exist some $m \in \mathbb{N}$ such that $a^m = e$. The fact that there exists a smallest such m, n say, follows from this, and we have shown (a) to be true.

In order to prove (b), note that we may write $m = o(a)q + r$ for some r satisfying $0 \leq r < o(a)$. Therefore

$$e = a^m = \left(a^{o(a)}\right)^q a^r = a^r.$$

From the definition of $o(a)$ and that of r, it must be the case that $r = 0$, as required. □

Research activity 6.1 You might like to pursue some more advanced reading on groups:

(a) An important result in group theory is *Lagrange's theorem*, which says that if H is a subgroup of a finite group G then the order of H divides the order of G. Make a careful study of a proof of this result, which may be found in [2], for example, and find out something about its applications. For example, why does Lagrange's theorem imply that the order of any element in a finite group divides the order of the group?

(b) Find out what it means for two groups to be *isomorphic*.

Finally, we discuss the notion of *generators* and *relations* with respect to groups. When considering the group $(G, \otimes_{10})$ given in challenge 6.3, we noted that the element 3 had order 4. Since there are only 4 elements in $(G, \otimes_{10})$, it must be the case that the powers of 3 provide all the elements of this group, namely $3^1 \equiv 3$, $3^2 \equiv 9$, $3^3 \equiv 7$ and $3^4 \equiv 1$ (all modulo 10). In such a case we term 3 a generator for $(G, \otimes_{10})$.

Chapter 6: Groups

Groups such as $(G, \otimes_{10})$ that can be generated by just one element are termed *cyclic*. In general though, it is not possible to generate a given group in this particularly simple way. In order to illustrate this, let us look at the group, H say, of functions used earlier to show that not all groups are abelian. This clearly cannot be generated by a single element since no elements have order 6. However, using the pair of generators f and g along with the three relations $f^2 = e$, $g^2 = e$ and $fgf = gfg$ (which are easily checked to be true), it is in fact possible to generate all of the 6 elements of H and no more.

Suppose in general that a group G can be generated by a subset X of its elements. Then a series of equations involving the elements of X and providing enough information to be able to construct the group table of G is called a set of defining relations for G. This idea has relevance to some of the work that will be carried out in chapters 8 and 9.

Exercise 6

1. We have already demonstrated the fact that the set of integers $\mathbb{Z}$ is a group with respect to addition. Show that $\mathbb{Z}$ is not a group with respect to multiplication.

2. (a) Let G be the subset of the rational numbers given by $\{3^m : m \in \mathbb{Z}\}$. Show that G is a group with respect to multiplication.
   (b) We know that $\mathbb{R}\backslash\{0\}$ is a group with respect to multiplication. Does it have G as a subgroup? Justify your answer.

3. (a) Obtain the set R_{14} of reduced residue classes modulo 14 (this should contain 6 elements).
   (b) Construct the group table of $(R_{14}, \otimes_{14})$.
   (c) For each element in $(R_{14}, \otimes_{14})$, find its order and its inverse.
   (d) Find all subgroups of $(R_{14}, \otimes_{14})$.

4. Construct the group table of G comprising the set $\{0, 1, 2, 3\}$ with respect to addition modulo 4. Find the order of each of the elements.

5. Find the order of each of the elements in the group of functions $\{e, f, g, h, i, j\}$ considered earlier in this chapter.

6. Let G be an abelian group with respect to some binary operation, where e is the identity of G. Show that, with respect to this binary operation, the set $H = \{x \in G : x^2 = e\}$ is a subgroup of G.

7. With the notation of theorem 6.5, show that $\{e, a, a^2, \ldots, a^{o(a)-1}\}$ is a subgroup of G of order $o(a)$, the cyclic group generated by a.

8. Consider the set $G_n = \{0, 1, 2, \ldots, n-1\}$ with respect to addition modulo n. This is another example of a finite cyclic group. Investigate the properties of such groups. Why are they called cyclic? What can we say about them when $n = p$ for some prime p? Do there exist infinite cyclic groups? If so, what do they look like? Are all their subgroups cyclic?

9. Let a be an element of a finite group G. Show that

$$o(a^m) = \frac{o(a)}{\gcd(m, o(a))}.$$

10. *If you have met matrices before:*

    Let G be the set of all 2×2 matrices

    $$\begin{pmatrix} a & b \\ c & d \end{pmatrix}$$

    such that $a, b, c, d \in \mathbb{R}$ and $ad \neq bc$.
    (a) Show that, with respect to matrix multiplication, G is a non-commutative group.
    (b) Find a finite subgroup of G with at least 4 elements.
    (c) Find an infinite subgroup of G.
    (d) Find a finite subgroup of G with exactly n elements.
    (e) Find an infinite subgroup of G in which every element has finite order.
    (f) Find an infinite subgroup of G in which every non-identity element does not have finite order.

Chapter 7

The roots of unity

As was mentioned in chapter 5, although Dirichlet's theorem is a statement about a property of the integers, it is necessary, in order to prove it, to utilise functions whose domains are the set of positive real numbers. Since the set of positive integers is a subset of the set of real numbers, it can be said that we have had to extend the domain in which the problem was posed in order to solve it. It will in fact be necessary, for the method of proof being used here, to go beyond even the real numbers to the complex numbers, denoted by $\mathbb{C}$. It is assumed that the reader has some basic familiarity with these numbers.

It was alluded to in chapter 6 that we will eventually be using some arithmetic functions called Dirichlet characters. They possess beautiful mathematical properties, called orthogonality relations, that make it possible to obtain certain sums over just the primes in any given arithmetic progression. It turns out that these functions, which we will meet in chapter 9, have certain complex numbers, called roots of unity, as outputs.

Let us consider the solutions to the equation $z^n = 1$. When $n = 1$ it is clear that $z = 1$ is a solution; furthermore, this is the *only* solution in this case. What about when $n = 2$? Well, $1^2 = (-1)^2 = 1$, so both $z = 1$ and $z = -1$ are solutions; indeed, they are the *only* solutions when $n = 2$. The Fundamental Theorem of Algebra (see research activity 7.1) tells us that any polynomial of degree n has n roots in $\mathbb{C}$, though not all of these are necessarily distinct. It turns out, however, that our equation always has n distinct roots, known as the nth *roots of unity*. The purpose of this chapter is to study some properties of these sets of numbers in preparation for the slightly more challenging mathematics to come.

When n is odd then 1 is the only real root and when $n \geq 2$ is even there are exactly two real roots, 1 and -1. In fact, the n roots are spaced evenly around a circle of radius 1 and centre 0 on an Argand diagram. The 6th roots of unity are shown in figure 7.1. In this case we can find them algebraically. If $z^6 = 1$ then

$$0 = z^6 - 1$$
$$= (z-1)(z+1)(z^2 - z + 1)(z^2 + z + 1)$$

so that

$$z = \pm 1, \ \frac{1 \pm i\sqrt{3}}{2}, \ \frac{-1 \pm i\sqrt{3}}{2}.$$

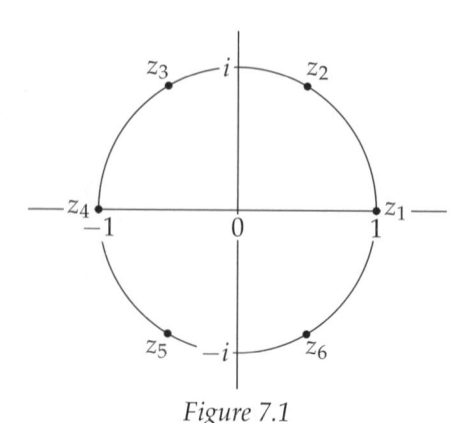

Figure 7.1

Table 7.1 lists all of the solutions to $z^n = 1$ for the first few values of n. You should check in each case that these numbers do indeed satisfy this equation. Let us consider the solution sets for $n = 2$, $n = 3$ and $n = 4$. Recall from chapter 6 that the set $\{1, -1\}$ is a group with respect to multiplication. It is a straightforward matter to check that

$$\left\{1, \ -\tfrac{1}{2} + \tfrac{\sqrt{3}}{2}i, \ -\tfrac{1}{2} - \tfrac{\sqrt{3}}{2}i\right\}$$

is also a group with respect to multiplication. In fact, both $-\tfrac{1}{2} + \tfrac{\sqrt{3}}{2}i$ and $-\tfrac{1}{2} - \tfrac{\sqrt{3}}{2}i$ generate the group, so it is cyclic. Moving on to $n = 4$, the set $\{1, i, -1, -i\}$ comprises another cyclic group, with both i and $-i$ generating the group.

n	nth roots of unity
1	1
2	$1, -1$
3	$1, -\frac{1}{2} + \frac{\sqrt{3}}{2}i, -\frac{1}{2} - \frac{\sqrt{3}}{2}i$
4	$1, i, -1, -i$

Table 7.1

Furthermore, we know from appendix D or challenge 7.1 that the non-real roots of $z^n = 1$ (those with non-zero imaginary part) always come in complex conjugate pairs. Thus if z_1 is a root of $z^n = 1$ then so is $\bar{z}_1$. This property can clearly be seen both in table 7.1 and in figure 7.1.

On adopting modulus-argument notation (see appendix D once more), the nth roots of unity are given by

$$\omega^k = \cos\frac{2\pi k}{n} + i\sin\frac{2\pi k}{n},$$

$k = 0, 1, 2, \ldots, n-1$, and we now look at this set of numbers, G_n say, with respect to multiplication. First,

$$\omega^k \omega^m = \omega^{k+m}$$
$$= \cos\frac{2\pi(k+m)}{n} + i\sin\frac{2\pi(k+m)}{n}.$$

Then, since

$$\cos\frac{2\pi(k+m)}{n} + i\sin\frac{2\pi(k+m)}{n} = \cos\frac{2\pi j}{n} + i\sin\frac{2\pi j}{n}$$

for some $j \in \{0, 1, 2, \ldots, n-1\}$, we see that G_n is closed. Also, the multiplication of complex numbers is associative. The number $\omega^0 = \cos 0 + i\sin 0 = 1$ serves as the identity and

$$\omega^k = \cos\frac{2\pi k}{n} + i\sin\frac{2\pi k}{n},$$

has inverse

$$\omega^{n-k} = \cos\frac{2\pi(n-k)}{n} + i\sin\frac{2\pi(n-k)}{n}.$$

It is therefore the case that G_n is a group with respect to multiplication, which we denote by $(G_n, \times)$.

Challenge 7.1 Show that if z is a complex root of unity then $\bar{z} = \frac{1}{z}$, so $\bar{z}$ is also a root of unity.

Next, from the exercises in chapter 6 we know that

$$o(\omega^k) = \frac{n}{\gcd(k,n)}.$$

Thus, in particular,

$$\omega = \cos\frac{2\pi}{n} + i\sin\frac{2\pi}{n}$$

is a generator for $(G_n, \times)$, which is therefore cyclic. If $\gcd(k,n) > 1$ then ω^k can be used to generate a subgroup of $(G_n, \times)$. For example, the element ω^2 of order 3 in the group comprising the sixth roots of unity $(G_6, \times)$ generates the subgroup $\{1, \omega^2, \omega^4\}$ with respect to multiplication.

Finally, it will be necessary to have reasonable fluency in using a particular type of inequality (and its generalisation) that often arises when manipulating expressions or solving problems involving the modulus function. In particular, we will be taking the modulus of sums of expressions involving nth roots of unity. The proof of this inequality is left as a challenge:

Challenge 7.2 Let $z_1, z_2 \in \mathbb{C}$. Prove that

$$|z_1 + z_2| \leq |z_1| + |z_2|,$$

and then go on to show that this result (called the *triangle inequality*) may be generalised to

$$|z_1 + z_2 + \ldots + z_n| \leq |z_1| + |z_2| + \ldots + |z_n|.$$

As the name would imply, the triangle inequality may be related to any triangle in the complex plane. It says essentially that the length of the longest side of a triangle never exceeds the combined length of the other two sides. To illustrate this let us consider the triangle in figure 7.2 with vertices z_a, z_b and z_c. Let $z_1 = z_a - z_c = 1 + 3i$ and $z_2 = z_c - z_b = 3 - i$.

Chapter 7: The roots of unity

Then the length of the side from z_b to z_a is given by

$$|z_1 + z_2| = |(1 + 3i) + (3 - i)|$$
$$= |4 + 2i|$$
$$= 2\sqrt{5}$$

while the length of the combined length of the other two sides is

$$|z_1| + |z_2| = |(1 + 3i)| + |(3 - i)|$$
$$= 2\sqrt{10}$$
$$> |z_1 + z_2|.$$

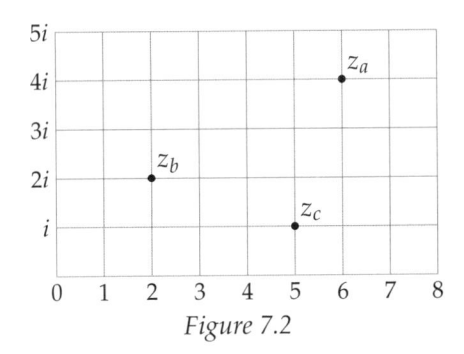

Figure 7.2

Research activity 7.1 The *Fundamental Theorem of Algebra* tells us about roots of polynomials. Suppose that $f(x)$ is some polynomial in x, possibly with complex coefficients, of degree at least 1. Then the theorem says that $f(x) = 0$ has at least one solution in $\mathbb{C}$. We say that the field of complex numbers is *algebraically closed*. An interesting fact about this theorem is that, in spite of its name, there is no purely algebraic proof.

A consequence of the Fundamental Theorem of Algebra is that $f(x) = 0$ has, accounting for possible repeated solutions, the same number of complex solutions as the degree of f.

Look into this theorem; either [10] or [24] might be a good start.

Exercise 7

1. Check that each of the 6th roots of unity, as calculated earlier in the chapter and displayed in figure 7.1, does indeed satisfy $z^6 = 1$.

2. If ω is a cube root of unity then find simpler expressions for both ω^{23} and $\frac{1}{\omega^{23}}$.

3. Let ω be one of the nth roots of unity. Obtain simpler expressions for each of the following:
   (a) $\overline{\omega}\omega$;
   (b) ω^{7n};
   (c) $|(2\omega)^k|$ where $k \in \mathbb{N}$;
   (d) $\omega^2 \omega^{n+1}$.

4. Find a systematic way of identifying all the subgroups of $(G_n, \times)$. Some of the material covered in chapter 6 might come in useful here, including Lagrange's theorem from research activity 6.1 on page 50.

5. (a) Show that $|z^n| = |z|^n$ for any $z \in \mathbb{C}$.
   (b) Hence show that if z is an nth root of unity then $|z| = 1$.

6. Prove that for any $n \in \mathbb{N}$ such that $n \geq 2$, the sum of all the nth roots of unity is always 0.

Chapter 8

An introduction to characters

It is necessary to have a reasonably good understanding of the mathematical ideas introduced in chapters 6 and 7 in order fully to appreciate what a character is. In very loose terms, a *character* is a function defined on the elements of a group in such a way as to endow it with particularly nice mathematical properties. In this book we are interested in a particular class of arithmetic functions that are derived from characters. These functions are called, appropriately enough, Dirichlet characters, and will be defined in chapter 9. In this chapter the notion of a group character is introduced.

Let us consider a simple example. We already know from chapter 6 (see challenge 6.4 on page 48, in particular) that $R_{12} = \{1, 5, 7, 11\}$ is a group with respect to multiplication modulo 12. The group table is given in table 8.1. We are looking for a function f from the elements of R_{12} to

$\otimes_{12}$	1	5	7	11
1	1	5	7	11
5	5	1	11	7
7	7	11	1	5
11	11	7	5	1

Table 8.1

the complex numbers which 'preserves multiplication' in the following sense. Let x and y be elements of R_{12}, whose product, modulo 12, is xy. Then we require that $f(xy) = f(x)f(y)$, where this, of course, is ordinary multiplication of complex numbers. One way of achieving this is to make $f(x) = 0$ for all x, but we do not want to consider this trivial case, and therefore exclude it. We are, however, interested in all other functions which preserve multiplication; we call this the *multiplicative property*.

One such function is rather obvious. Indeed, $f_1 : R_{12} \to \mathbb{C}$ defined by $f_1(x) = 1$ for all $x \in R_{12}$ is certainly multiplicative. Another function f_2 given by $f_2(1) = 1$, $f_2(5) = -1$, $f_2(7) = 1$ and $f_2(11) = -1$ also satisfies the criteria. For example, $f_2(7 \otimes_{12} 5) = f_2(11) = -1$ and $f_2(7)f_2(5) = 1 \times -1 = -1$, and similarly for all other possible pairs of elements. Further exploration reveals two more functions, f_3 and f_4, and no others. These four functions are called the *characters* of the group $(R_{12}, \otimes_{12})$. They are summarised in the *character table* given in table 8.2.

n	$f_1(n)$	$f_2(n)$	$f_3(n)$	$f_4(n)$
1	1	1	1	1
5	1	−1	1	−1
7	1	1	−1	−1
11	1	−1	−1	1

Table 8.2

We can now give a formal definition of a character. For our purposes we are only concerned with residue class groups, but definition 8.1 can easily be extended to any finite group.

Definition 8.1 *The function $f : R_k \to \mathbb{C}$ is a character of $(R_k, \otimes_k)$ if:*
(a) $f(xy) = f(x)f(y)$ *for any $x, y \in R_k$, where the product xy is carried out modulo k while $f(x)f(y)$ is performed using normal multiplication;*
(b) *there is at least one element $x \in R_k$ such that $f(x) \neq 0$.*

Some facts about characters are immediate. Suppose that f is a character of $(R_k, \otimes_k)$. If a is an element of $(R_k, \otimes_k)$ for which $f(a) \neq 0$ then, from
$$f(a) = f(1 \otimes_k a) = f(1)f(a),$$
we see that $f(1) = 1$. Additionally, if b is any element of $(R_k, \otimes_k)$ then

Chapter 8: An introduction to characters

there exists a least positive integer n such that $b^n = 1$. Therefore

$$1 = f(1) = f(b^n) = f(b)^n,$$

showing that $f(b)$ is an nth root of unity. In fact, since R_k has order $\phi(k)$ (from challenge 6.4 on page 48), it follows (research activity 6.1 on page 50) that n here is a factor of $\phi(k)$.

It can also be shown that, with respect to a particular binary operation, the characters of $(R_k, \otimes_k)$ form a group which is closed under complex conjugation. This result will be proved in chapter 9, and we simply offer a foretaste here. Note that every group G does indeed possess at least one character f_1, namely the one for which $f_1(x) = 1$ for all elements $x \in G$. This particular character is called the *principal character*, and will be shown to be the identity of the group. The binary operation in question is a type of product. If g and h are two characters of $(R_k, \otimes_k)$ then gh is given by $gh(x) = g(x)h(x)$ for all $x \in R_k$.

We may next ask, with regard to the previous example, whether it is a coincidence that the number of characters is the same as the order of the group? In order to explore this possibility let us study the group $(R_{14}, \otimes_{14})$. This has six elements given by $R_{14} = \{1, 3, 5, 9, 11, 13\}$. We will show, via a particular construction, that $(R_{14}, \otimes_{14})$ does actually have six distinct characters, the same as the number of elements in the group. It is easily checked that the elements 3, 5, 9, 11 and 13 have orders 6, 6, 3, 3 and 2, respectively.

Let f be a character of $(R_{14}, \otimes_{14})$. Then, for any $x \in R_{14}$, $f(x)$ is one of the sixth roots of unity given by $\{\omega^k : k = 0, 1, \ldots, 5\}$, where

$$\omega = \cos\frac{2\pi}{6} + i\sin\frac{2\pi}{6}$$
$$= \frac{1}{2} + \frac{\sqrt{3}}{2}i.$$

Let us consider $f(3)$ in particular. The element 3 has order 6 and is therefore a generator for $(R_{14}, \otimes_{14})$. Thus, via the multiplicative property, $f(3)$ determines $f(x)$ for each $x \in R_{14}$. For example, if $f(3) = \omega^5$ we have

$$f(13) = f(3^3)$$
$$= f(3)^3$$
$$= \omega^{15}$$
$$= \omega^3.$$

Then, noting that each of the six distinct sixth roots of unity may be assigned to $f(3)$, it follows that $(R_{14}, \otimes_{14})$ has 6 characters. Table 8.3 summarises the situation; note that $5 = 3^5, 9 = 3^2, 11 = 3^4$ and $13 = 3^3$.

n	$f_1(n)$	$f_2(n)$	$f_3(n)$	$f_4(n)$	$f_5(n)$	$f_6(n)$
1	1	1	1	1	1	1
3	1	ω	ω^2	ω^3	ω^4	ω^5
5	1	ω^5	ω^4	ω^3	ω^2	ω
9	1	ω^2	ω^4	1	ω^2	ω^4
11	1	ω^4	ω^2	1	ω^4	ω^2
13	1	ω^3	1	ω^3	1	ω^3

Table 8.3

This was a rather straightforward example since the group possessed a single generator. When this is not the case we need to employ a set of generators in order to construct the characters; generators and relations were discussed briefly at the end of chapter 6. Let us reconsider the group $(R_{12}, \otimes_{12})$ for which we obtained the characters via a trial-and-error approach. It is easily checked that this group does not have a single generator. In fact the elements 5, 7 and 11 each have order 2. However, $\{5,7\}$ is a set of generators for $(R_{12}, \otimes_{12})$. If f is a character then we may assign either 1 or -1 to $f(5)$ and similarly for $f(7)$. There are thus $2 \times 2 = 4$ possible ways of assigning values to the pair $f(5)$ and $f(7)$. Either $f(5) = f(7) = 1$, $f(5) = 1$ and $f(7) = -1$, $f(5) = 1$ and $f(7) = 1$ or $f(5) = f(7) = -1$. The multiplicative property in conjunction with the the fact that $\{5,7\}$ is a set of generators for $(R_{12}, \otimes_{12})$ leads to the character table displayed earlier. Note that the set of generators for a finite group is not in general unique. You will see, for example, that $\{5, 11\}$ is also a set of generators for $(R_{12}, \otimes_{12})$, as is $\{7, 11\}$.

A slightly more ambitious example is the group $(R_{15}, \otimes_{15})$ with elements $R_{15} = \{1, 2, 4, 7, 8, 11, 13, 14\}$. Once again there is no single generating element, but $\{2, 14\}$ is a set of generators. The orders of 2 and 14 are 4 and 2, respectively. By assigning suitable values to $f(2)$ and $f(14)$, the character table for $(R_{15}, \otimes_{15})$ may be constructed. This group does indeed possess 8 distinct characters. Another set of generators for $(R_{15}, \otimes_{15})$ is $\{11, 13\}$.

Chapter 8: An introduction to characters 63

Challenge 8.1   Construct the character table for $(R_{15}, \otimes_{15})$.

Before moving on, it is worth trying out some examples of your own and also considering the situation in greater generality. Remember that the groups $(R_k, \otimes_k)$ we have been looking at here are all abelian. There is in fact a general theorem in this regard, and this is the object of the following research activity.

Research activity 8.1   A formal proof of the fact that a finite abelian group of order n has exactly n distinct characters appears in [1, theorem 6.8], for example. Try to locate a proof of this result and study it in detail. This is a good way to find out about the structural properties of finite abelian groups.

Chapter 9

Dirichlet characters and their orthogonality relations

In chapter 8 we studied characters of groups of the form $(R_k, \otimes_k)$. These groups of reduced residue classes modulo k were shown in challenge 6.4 on page 48 to possess $\phi(k)$ elements. Furthermore, in each of the examples covered in chapter 8 it was found that they also have $\phi(k)$ characters; the reader was indeed invited in research activity 8.1 on page 63 to seek out a proof of the fact that this was no coincidence. We now consider the so-called orthogonality relations of these characters, noting that the arithmetic functions we term Dirichlet characters, which will be used to great effect in our proof of Dirichlet's theorem, are derived from them later in this chapter.

Let us give an example to explain the idea of an orthogonality relation. We already know that the character table for $(R_{14}, \otimes_{14})$ is the one shown in table 9.1. It is easy to show that each of the rows has a sum of zero, except for the first one, which has a sum of 6, and likewise for the columns. Let a_{lm} denote the element in the lth row and mth column of table 9.1. For the ith and jth rows, $(a_{i1}, a_{i2}, a_{i3}, a_{i4}, a_{i5}, a_{i6})$ and $(a_{j1}, a_{j2}, a_{j3}, a_{j4}, a_{j5}, a_{j6})$, in the table we define their 'product' as

$$a_{i1}\bar{a}_{j1} + a_{i2}\bar{a}_{j2} + a_{i3}\bar{a}_{j3} + a_{i4}\bar{a}_{j4} + a_{i5}\bar{a}_{j5} + a_{i6}\bar{a}_{j6},$$

where, as usual, $\bar{a}_{lm}$ denotes the complex conjugate of a_{lm}. This might in fact remind you a little bit of the scalar or dot product of two vectors,

n	$f_1(n)$	$f_2(n)$	$f_3(n)$	$f_4(n)$	$f_5(n)$	$f_6(n)$
1	1	1	1	1	1	1
3	1	ω	ω^2	ω^3	ω^4	ω^5
5	1	ω^5	ω^4	ω^3	ω^2	ω
9	1	ω^2	ω^4	1	ω^2	ω^4
11	1	ω^4	ω^2	1	ω^4	ω^2
13	1	ω^3	1	ω^3	1	ω^3

Table 9.1

except we now seem to be in more than three dimensions. We have, for example,

$$a_{21}\bar{a}_{31} + a_{22}\bar{a}_{32} + a_{23}\bar{a}_{33} + a_{24}\bar{a}_{34} + a_{25}\bar{a}_{35} + a_{26}\bar{a}_{36}$$
$$= 1 \times 1 + \omega\overline{\omega^5} + \omega^2\overline{\omega^4} + \omega^3\overline{\omega^3} + \omega^4\overline{\omega^2} + \omega^5\overline{\omega}$$
$$= 1 \times 1 + \omega\omega + \omega^2\omega^2 + \omega^3\omega^3 + \omega^4\omega^4 + \omega^5\omega^5$$
$$= 1 + \omega^2 + \omega^4 + \omega^6 + \omega^8 + \omega^{10}$$
$$= 1 + \omega^2 + \omega^4 + 1 + \omega^2 + \omega^4$$
$$= 0$$

while

$$a_{31}\bar{a}_{31} + a_{32}\bar{a}_{32} + a_{33}\bar{a}_{33} + a_{34}\bar{a}_{34} + a_{35}\bar{a}_{35} + a_{36}\bar{a}_{36}$$
$$= 1 \times 1 + \omega^5\overline{\omega^5} + \omega^4\overline{\omega^4} + \omega^3\overline{\omega^3} + \omega^2\overline{\omega^2} + \omega\overline{\omega}$$
$$= 1 \times 1 + \omega^5\omega + \omega^4\omega^2 + \omega^3\omega^3 + \omega^2\omega^4 + \omega\omega^5$$
$$= 1 + \omega^6 + \omega^6 + \omega^6 + \omega^6 + \omega^6$$
$$= 6.$$

It may easily be checked that the product is 6 if the rows are the same (so that $i = j$) or 0 if the rows are distinct ($i \neq j$). This is called the *orthogonality relation* for the characters of $(R_{14}, \otimes_{14})$. In order to prove a generalisation of this, and hence make further progress, we need the notion of the complex conjugate of a character:

Definition 9.1 *The complex conjugate of the character f, denoted $\bar{f}$, is defined*

Chapter 9: Dirichlet characters and their orthogonality relations

by
$$\overline{f}(a) = \overline{f(a)}$$
for each $a \in R_k$.

If f is a character then so is $\overline{f}$. To see this, note first that from the definition of a character there is some $a \in R_k$ such that $f(a) \neq 0$. Thus $\overline{f}(a) = \overline{f(a)} \neq 0$. Second, since $f(ab) = f(a)f(b)$ for any $a, b \in R_k$, it is the case that

$$\begin{aligned}\overline{f}(ab) &= \overline{f(ab)} \\ &= \overline{f(a)f(b)} \\ &= \overline{f}(a)\overline{f}(b),\end{aligned}$$

as required.

We now possess the notation to allow us to state an important general result. For any $i, j \in R_k$, the orthogonality relation for the characters of $(R_k, \otimes_k)$ is as follows:

$$\sum_{m=1}^{\phi(k)} f_m(i)\overline{f}_m(j) = \begin{cases} \phi(k) & \text{if } i = j \\ 0 & \text{otherwise.} \end{cases} \tag{9.1}$$

The aim of the much of the remainder of the chapter is to prove result (9.1). We start by recalling the comment in chapter 8 that this set of characters form a group with respect to a particular binary operation. We formalise here the definition of this binary operation and prove that the characters do indeed form a group with respect to it.

Definition 9.2 *The 'product' of two characters f_i and f_j is given by*

$$(f_i f_j)(a) = f_i(a) f_j(a)$$

for each $a \in R_k$.

Theorem 9.3 *The characters of $(R_k, \otimes_k)$ form a group with respect to the product given by definition 9.2.*

PROOF First note that $(f_i f_j)(1) = f_i(1) f_j(1) = 1$ so there does exist at least one element $a \in R_k$ such that $(f_i f_j)(a) \neq 0$. Next, for $a, b \in R_k$ it follows from definition 9.2 that

$$\begin{aligned}(f_if_j)(a)(f_if_j)(b) &= f_i(a)f_j(a)f_i(b)f_j(b) \\ &= f_i(ab)f_j(ab) \\ &= (f_if_j)(ab),\end{aligned}$$

which shows that f_if_j is indeed a character of $(R_k, \otimes_k)$, and hence that the binary operation is closed. Furthermore, it is clear that the identity of this group is the principal character f_1, but what about inverses? Well, for f_j to be the inverse of f_i we require f_if_j to be the identity, f_1. In other words, it must be the case that

$$\begin{aligned}f_i(a)f_j(a) &= (f_if_j)(a) \\ &= f_1(a) \\ &= 1,\end{aligned}$$

for each $a \in R_k$. The inverse f_i^{-1} would then be given by $f_i^{-1}(a) = \frac{1}{f_i(a)}$ for each $a \in R_k$, so long as this is actually a character. Since $f_i(a)$ is always a complex root of unity, it follows, from challenge 7.1, that f_i^{-1} is given by $f_i^{-1}(a) = \overline{f}_i(a)$ for each $a \in R_k$. However, we already know, by way of the discussion following definition 9.1, that if f is a character then so is $\overline{f}$. Thus, with respect to the product given by definition 9.2, this set of characters does indeed form a group. ∎

Next, although we know that

$$\sum_{m=1}^{\phi(k)} f_m(1) = \phi(k),$$

is there anything that can be said about

$$\sum_{m=1}^{\phi(k)} f_m(a)$$

when $a \neq 1$? In fact it turns out that this latter sum is equal to zero, as we now show.

When $a \neq 1$ there exists some $q \in \mathbb{N}$ with $2 \leq q \leq \phi(k)$ such that $f_q(a) \neq 1$. In order to see this, note that the process by which the character

Chapter 9: Dirichlet characters and their orthogonality relations   69

table for $(R_k, \otimes_k)$ is constructed means that, with the complex root of unity given by

$$\zeta = \cos\frac{2\pi}{\phi(k)} + i\sin\frac{2\pi}{\phi(k)},$$

each of the numbers in the set

$$\left\{\zeta^{\frac{j\phi(k)}{o(a)}} : j = 0, 1, \ldots, o(a) - 1\right\}$$

appears in the row for a, where $o(a)$ is the order of a. Thus, because $a \neq 1$ implies that $o(a) > 1$, it is indeed possible to find a q such that $f_q(a) \neq 1$. Since the characters form a group with respect to the product given by definition 9.2, the set $\{f_1, f_2, \ldots, f_{\phi(k)}\}$ is the same as the set $\{f_1 f_q, f_2 f_q, \ldots, f_{\phi(k)} f_q\}$. This is essentially due to the fact that a cancellation law exists for all groups; see also challenge 6.6 and theorem C.2 on page 49 and on page 162. Note though that the equality of these two sets certainly does not imply that $f_1 f_q = f_1$, $f_2 f_q = f_2$, and so on.

As a consequence of the discussion in the previous paragraph it now follows that

$$\sum_{m=1}^{\phi(k)} f_m(a) = \sum_{m=1}^{\phi(k)} (f_m f_q)(a)$$

$$= \sum_{m=1}^{\phi(k)} f_m(a) f_q(a)$$

$$= f_q(a) \sum_{m=1}^{\phi(k)} f_m(a),$$

from which it can be seen, since $f_q(a) \neq 1$, that

$$\sum_{m=1}^{\phi(k)} f_m(a) = 0, \qquad (9.2)$$

as promised. This simply demonstrates the truth of the property we noticed earlier concerning row sums of character tables, namely that, other than the one corresponding to $a = 1$, the row sums are zero.

Now let $i, j \in R_k$ be such that $i = j$. Then

$$\sum_{m=1}^{\phi(k)} f_m(i)\overline{f}_m(j) = \sum_{m=1}^{\phi(k)} f_m(i)\overline{f}_m(i)$$

$$= \sum_{m=1}^{\phi(k)} \frac{f_m(i)}{f_m(i)}$$

$$= \phi(k).$$

Suppose, on the other hand, that $i \neq j$. Then there exists a unique element j^{-1} in R_k, the inverse of j, such that $j^{-1}j \equiv 1 \pmod{k}$. Therefore,

$$1 = f_m(1) = f_m(j^{-1}j) = f_m(j^{-1})f_m(j),$$

and hence

$$\sum_{m=1}^{\phi(k)} f_m(i)\overline{f}_m(j) = \sum_{m=1}^{\phi(k)} \frac{f_m(i)}{f_m(j)}$$

$$= \sum_{m=1}^{\phi(k)} f_m(i)f_m(j^{-1})$$

$$= \sum_{m=1}^{\phi(k)} f_m(ij^{-1}).$$

However, since $i \neq j$, it follows that $ij^{-1} \not\equiv 1 \pmod{k}$. Thus, from result (9.2), we obtain our sought-after result (9.1), namely

$$\sum_{m=1}^{\phi(k)} f_m(i)\overline{f}_m(j) = 0.$$

Each character f does actually give rise, in a very natural way, to an arithmetic function χ_f, defined as follows:

Definition 9.4 *The character f of $(R_k, \otimes_k)$ induces a* Dirichlet character *modulo k defined by*

$$\chi_f(n) = \begin{cases} f(\hat{n}) & \text{if } \gcd(n, k) = 1 \\ 0 & \text{if } \gcd(n, k) > 1, \end{cases}$$

where $n \in \mathbb{N}$ and $\hat{n}$ is the unique element of the set $\{0, 1, 2, \ldots, k-1\}$ such that $\hat{n} \equiv n \pmod{k}$. In other words, $\hat{n}$ is n reduced modulo k; see appendix C.

Chapter 9: Dirichlet characters and their orthogonality relations   71

It is important to be clear about the range and domain of f and χ_f. While both functions map into the set of complex numbers $\mathbb{C}$, they have different domains. In fact we have $f : R_k \to \mathbb{C}$ and $\chi_f : \mathbb{N} \to \mathbb{C}$. In other words, χ_f is defined on all positive integers while f is defined on only a restricted (and finite) subset of them.

Challenge 9.1   Let χ_f be a Dirichlet character modulo k. Show that χ_f is a periodic function with period k in the sense that $\chi_f(k+n) = \chi_f(n)$ for all positive integers n.

It is clear, from definition 9.4 and the properties of characters discussed in chapter 8, that a Dirichlet character is completely multiplicative. Furthermore, from what has gone before, there are $\phi(k)$ distinct Dirichlet characters modulo k. The characters of $(R_k, \otimes_k)$ and the Dirichlet characters modulo k they induce may thus be denoted by $f_1, f_2, \ldots, f_{\phi(k)}$ and $\chi_1, \chi_2, \ldots, \chi_{\phi(k)}$, respectively, where χ_1 is the *principal Dirichlet character* modulo k defined by

$$\chi_1(n) = \begin{cases} 1 & \text{if } \gcd(n,k) = 1 \\ 0 & \text{if } \gcd(n,k) > 1. \end{cases}$$

In order to illustrate this, the character f_3 of the group $(R_{14}, \otimes_{14})$ studied earlier gives rise to the Dirichlet character χ_3 for which, since $\gcd(6, 14) \neq 1$, $\chi_3(6 + 14n) = 0$ for $n = 0, 1, 2, \ldots$. Thus

$$\chi_3(6) = \chi_3(20) = \chi_3(34) = \ldots = 0.$$

Similarly,

$$\chi_3(7) = \chi_3(21) = \chi_3(35) = \ldots = 0,$$

and so on. On the other hand, since $\gcd(9, 14) = 1$ and $f_3(9) = \omega^4$, it follows that

$$\chi_3(9) = \chi_3(23) = \chi_3(37) = \ldots = \omega^4.$$

From result (9.1) it is a reasonably straightforward matter to obtain the following orthogonality relation for the Dirichlet characters. For any $i, j \in \mathbb{N}$;

$$\sum_{m=1}^{\phi(k)} \chi_m(i) \overline{\chi}_m(j) = \begin{cases} \phi(k) & \text{if } \gcd(i,k) = 1 \text{ and } i \equiv j \pmod{k} \\ 0 & \text{otherwise,} \end{cases} \quad (9.3)$$

where $\overline{\chi}_m$ represents the Dirichlet character such that $\overline{\chi}_m(n) = \overline{\chi_m(n)}$ for each $n \in \mathbb{N}$.

Before showing that result (9.1) implies the truth of result (9.3), it is worth noting once again the fact that the characters of $(R_k, \otimes_k)$ appearing in result (9.1) have as their domain the finite set R_k, while the Dirichlet characters have as theirs the set of positive integers $\mathbb{N}$.

Now to prove result (9.3). First, it follows from definition 9.4 that the sum on the left-hand side of result (9.3) is equal to zero when $\gcd(i,k) > 1$. Let us suppose then that $\gcd(i,k) = 1$. It is true that $\gcd(i,k) = 1$ if, and only if, $\hat{\imath} \in R_k$, where the notation $\hat{n}$ is as given in definition 9.4. Therefore, from definition 9.4 and result (9.1), it follows that the sum on the left-hand side of result (9.3) is equal to $\phi(k)$ when $\hat{\imath} = \hat{\jmath}$, and zero otherwise. Result (9.3) follows since $\hat{\imath} = \hat{\jmath}$ if, and only if, $i \equiv j \pmod{k}$. This relation will certainly be put to extremely good use in later chapters.

Result (9.1) is concerned with the orthogonality property of rows of character tables. We will also need the following result associated with the orthogonality of columns. For any non-principal character f_m,

$$\sum_{n=1}^{\phi(k)} f_m(a_n) = 0, \qquad (9.4)$$

where $a_n \in R_k, n = 1, 2, \ldots, \phi(k)$. Let us prove this. First, since f_m is not a principal character, it must be the case that $f_m(a_i) \neq 1$ for some i. On using theorem C.2 on page 162, we have

$$\sum_{n=1}^{\phi(k)} f_m(a_n) = \sum_{n=1}^{\phi(k)} f_m(a_i a_n).$$

However,

$$\sum_{n=1}^{\phi(k)} f_m(a_i a_n) = f_m(a_i) \sum_{n=1}^{\phi(k)} f_m(a_n),$$

which implies, since $f_m(a_i) \neq 1$, the truth of result (9.4).

Challenge 9.2 Statement (9.1) gives the orthogonality property for rows of the character table. Establish the analogous orthogonality relations for the columns:

$$\sum_{i=1}^{\phi(k)} f_m(a_i)\overline{f_n}(a_i) = \begin{cases} \phi(k) & \text{if } m = n \\ 0 & \text{otherwise,} \end{cases}$$

where $R_k = \{a_1, a_2, \ldots, a_{\phi(k)}\}$.

The concept of characters applies to groups in general, not just to the groups $(R_k, \otimes_k)$ we have considered. For those interested in carrying out further reading on characters see [1].

Exercise 9

1. Verify that the orthogonality relations hold for the character table of the group $(R_{12}, \otimes_{12})$.

2. (a) Find all Dirichlet characters of the group $(R_{20}, \otimes_{20})$.
   (b) Demonstrate the orthogonality relations of these characters.

3. Suppose that χ is a non-principal Dirichlet character modulo k. Let $i, j \in \mathbb{N}$ such that $i < j$. Prove that

$$\left|\sum_{n=i}^{j} \chi(n)\right| \leq \frac{\phi(k)}{2}.$$

4. We already know that any Dirichlet character χ_f modulo k is periodic with period k; see challenge 9.1.
   (a) It is possible for χ_f also to possess a smaller period. Find a specific example for which this is the case.
   (b) Suppose that the smallest period of χ_f is m. Show that m is a factor of k.
   (c) Let $k \in \mathbb{N}$ be *square-free* (in other words, k has no square factors other than 1). Show that in this case k is the smallest period of χ_f.

Chapter 10

Dirichlet *L*-functions

The following two infinite series play a leading role in the proof:

$$L_m = \sum_{n=1}^{\infty} \frac{\chi_m(n)}{n} \quad \text{and} \quad L'_m = -\sum_{n=1}^{\infty} \frac{\chi_m(n)\log n}{n}. \tag{10.1}$$

They are actually special cases of the *Dirichlet L-functions*, but are sufficient for our purposes. Note that L_m and L'_m are simply functions of the character $\chi_m(n)$. In situations where the sums involve a character χ without a subscript, L and L' may be used without ambiguity. The precise role that L_m and L'_m will play in the proof is impossible to explain in a sentence or two. Their real point will become apparent when we get to chapter 16.

In discussing these series, we will be making use of the Cauchy convergence criterion for infinite series. This will be found in appendix A, and you are strongly advised to make sure that you understand this before you embark on the arguments in this chapter.

For any particular character, L_m is an infinite series that either converges or diverges, and similarly for L'_m. If L_m, for example, does converge then we can write $L_m = c$ for some constant c that may possibly be complex. Let us first consider the sum L_1 involving the principal Dirichlet character modulo k for some $k \in \mathbb{N}$:

$$L_1 = \sum_{n=1}^{\infty} \frac{\chi_1(n)}{n}.$$

We know that $\chi_1(n) = 1$ if $\gcd(n,k) = 1$, and $\chi_1(n) = 0$ otherwise. Thus if $k = 10$, for example, then

$$\sum_{n=1}^{\infty} \frac{\chi_1(n)}{n} = 1 + \frac{1}{3} + \frac{1}{7} + \frac{1}{9} + \frac{1}{11} + \cdots$$

$$> \frac{1}{11} + \frac{1}{21} + \frac{1}{31} + \frac{1}{41} + \cdots$$

$$> \frac{1}{11}\left(1 + \frac{1}{2} + \frac{1}{3} + \frac{1}{4} + \cdots\right).$$

This tells us, from the result on the harmonic series in chapter 3, that L_1 diverges in this case. More generally, in the modulo k case,

$$\sum_{n=1}^{\infty} \frac{\chi_1(n)}{n} > \sum_{m=1}^{\infty} \frac{1}{mk+1}$$

$$> \frac{1}{k+1}\left(1 + \frac{1}{2} + \frac{1}{3} + \frac{1}{4} + \cdots\right),$$

showing that L_1 diverges for any $k \in \mathbb{N}$. This implies that L'_1 also diverges since

$$\frac{\chi_1(n) \log n}{n} > \frac{\chi_1(n)}{n}$$

for all $n \geq 3$.

On the other hand, it will in fact be shown in this chapter that L_m and L'_m both converge for all non-principal characters. In what follows it may be assumed that $m > 1$ and hence that χ_m is a non-principal Dirichlet character modulo k.

Before going any further, it is useful to try to evaluate L_m for some special cases. Consider the group $(R_8, \otimes_8)$ with respect to multiplication modulo 8. As you should check, the character table for this group is given in table 10.1.

n	$f_1(n)$	$f_2(n)$	$f_3(n)$	$f_4(n)$
1	1	1	1	1
3	1	−1	1	−1
5	1	1	−1	−1
7	1	−1	−1	1

Table 10.1

It follows from this that

$$L_2 = 1 - \frac{1}{3} + \frac{1}{5} - \frac{1}{7} + \frac{1}{9} - \frac{1}{11} + \cdots$$

$$= \sum_{k=0}^{\infty} \left(\frac{1}{4k+1} - \frac{1}{4k+3} \right)$$

$$= \sum_{k=0}^{\infty} \frac{(-1)^k}{2k+1}$$

$$= \frac{\pi}{4}.$$

Challenge 10.1

(a) Show that

$$\sum_{k=0}^{\infty} \frac{(-1)^k}{2k+1} = \frac{\pi}{4}.$$

As a hint, evaluate the integral

$$\int_0^1 \frac{1}{1+x^2} \, dx$$

via two different methods, one of which utilises a suitable binomial expansion. Incidentally, the above series is known as *Gregory's series*, named after the British mathematician and astronomer James Gregory (1638–1675).

(b) Now evaluate the sum L_3. In order to do this you can use the integral

$$\int_0^1 \frac{1+x^{-2}}{x^2+x^{-2}} \, dx,$$

along with the substitution $u = x - \frac{1}{x}$.

(c) Similarly, obtain L_4 by using

$$\int_0^1 \frac{x^{-2} - 1}{x^2 + x^{-2}} \, dx,$$

and putting $u = x + \frac{1}{x}$.

From challenge 10.1 you will have found that

$$L_3 = 1 + \frac{1}{3} - \frac{1}{5} - \frac{1}{7} + \frac{1}{9} + \frac{1}{11} - \frac{1}{13} - \frac{1}{15} + \cdots$$

$$= \sum_{k=0}^{\infty} \left(\frac{1}{8k+1} + \frac{1}{8k+3} - \frac{1}{8k+5} - \frac{1}{8k+7} \right)$$

$$= \frac{\pi}{2\sqrt{2}}$$

and

$$L_4 = 1 - \frac{1}{3} - \frac{1}{5} + \frac{1}{7} + \frac{1}{9} - \frac{1}{11} - \frac{1}{13} + \frac{1}{15} + \cdots$$

$$= \sum_{k=0}^{\infty} \left(\frac{1}{8k+1} - \frac{1}{8k+3} - \frac{1}{8k+5} + \frac{1}{8k+7} \right)$$

$$= \frac{\log(1+\sqrt{2})}{\sqrt{2}}.$$

Thus, for this special case at least, all the Dirichlet L-functions corresponding to non-principal characters do indeed converge. In the exercise at the end of this chapter, you will have the opportunity to carry out similar calculations for some complex-valued non-principal characters.

Let us now get on with the job of obtaining some useful results concerning our two infinite series L_m and L'_m. As usual, let $R_k = \{a_1, a_2, \ldots, a_{\phi(k)}\}$ be the set of $\phi(k)$ positive integers that are both less than k and coprime to it. From the definition of a Dirichlet character (see definition 9.4) $\chi_m(n) \neq 0$ if, and only if, $\gcd(n, k) = 1$. This, along with (9.4), gives

$$\sum_{n=1}^{k} \chi_m(n) = \begin{cases} \phi(k) & \text{when } m = 1 \\ 0 & \text{otherwise.} \end{cases}$$

Hence, from the periodicity of Dirichlet characters discussed in chapter 9, it follows, bearing in mind that we are only considering non-principal characters here, that

$$\sum_{n=1}^{k} \chi_m(n) = \sum_{n=k+1}^{2k} \chi_m(n) = \sum_{n=2k+1}^{3k} \chi_m(n) = \cdots = 0.$$

Also, if $n \equiv a \pmod{k}$ for some $a \in R_k$, then $|\chi_m(n)| = 1$ since $\chi_m(n)$ is a root of unity. Combining this both with the above result and the triangle

Chapter 10: Dirichlet L-functions   79

inequality from challenge 7.2 shows, on defining $A(x)$ by
$$A(x) = \sum_{n \leq x} \chi_m(n)$$
for $x \in \mathbb{R}$, that $|A(x)| \leq \phi(k)$. (Note, incidentally, that in question 2 of chapter 9 the somewhat sharper result $|A(x)| \leq \frac{1}{2}\phi(k)$ was obtained.) Using 'big oh' notation, we may write this inequality as $A(x) = O(1)$.

We are now in a position to relate the sums
$$L_m \quad \text{and} \quad \sum_{n \leq x} \frac{\chi_m(n)}{n}.$$

Let x and y be real numbers such that $0 < x < y$, with a and b denoting the largest integers not exceeding x and y respectively. Noting that $A(n) - A(n-1) = \chi_m(n)$, after some manipulation we get

$$\sum_{x < n \leq y} \frac{\chi_m(n)}{n} = \sum_{n=a+1}^{b} \frac{\chi_m(n)}{n}$$
$$= \sum_{n=a+1}^{b} \frac{A(n) - A(n-1)}{n}$$
$$= \sum_{n=a+1}^{b} \frac{A(n)}{n} - \sum_{n=a+1}^{b} \frac{A(n-1)}{n}$$
$$= \sum_{n=a+1}^{b} \frac{A(n)}{n} - \sum_{n=a}^{b-1} \frac{A(n)}{n+1}$$
$$= \sum_{n=a+1}^{b-1} A(n)\left(\frac{1}{n} - \frac{1}{n+1}\right) + \frac{A(b)}{b} - \frac{A(a)}{a+1}.$$

However, on using the result of challenge 7.2 and the fact that $|\chi_m(n)| = 1$ or $|\chi_m(n)| = 0$, we obtain

$$\left| \sum_{n=a+1}^{b-1} A(n)\left(\frac{1}{n} - \frac{1}{n+1}\right) \right| \leq \sum_{n=a+1}^{b-1} \left| A(n)\left(\frac{1}{n} - \frac{1}{n+1}\right) \right|$$
$$= \sum_{n=a+1}^{b-1} |A(n)| \left(\frac{1}{n} - \frac{1}{n+1}\right)$$
$$\leq M \sum_{n=a+1}^{b-1} \left(\frac{1}{n} - \frac{1}{n+1}\right),$$

for some positive real number M that, since $A(x) = O(1)$, does not depend on a or b. This gives

$$\left| \sum_{n=a+1}^{b-1} A(n) \left(\frac{1}{n} - \frac{1}{n+1} \right) \right|$$
$$\leq M \left\{ \left(\frac{1}{a+1} - \frac{1}{a+2} \right) + \left(\frac{1}{a+2} - \frac{1}{a+3} \right) + \cdots + \left(\frac{1}{b-1} - \frac{1}{b} \right) \right\}$$
$$= M \left\{ \frac{1}{a+1} - \frac{1}{b} \right\},$$

where we see another example of a sum 'telescoping' to leave a particularly simple result. Therefore

$$\left| \sum_{x<n\leq y} \frac{\chi_m(n)}{n} \right| \leq M \left\{ \frac{1}{a+1} - \frac{1}{b} \right\} + \left| \frac{A(b)}{b} \right| + \left| \frac{A(a)}{a+1} \right|$$
$$\leq M \left\{ \frac{1}{a+1} - \frac{1}{b} \right\} + \frac{M}{b} + \frac{M}{a+1}$$
$$= \frac{2M}{a+1},$$

showing that

$$\sum_{x<n\leq y} \frac{\chi_m(n)}{n} = O\left(\frac{1}{x} \right).$$

This result actually tells us, via the Cauchy convergence criterion from appendix A, that L_m converges.

Challenge 10.2 Figure out how to apply the Cauchy convergence criterion to show that the relation

$$\sum_{x<n\leq y} \frac{\chi_m(n)}{n} = O\left(\frac{1}{x} \right)$$

implies that L_m converges.

Also, since

$$\sum_{n=1}^{\infty} \frac{\chi_m(n)}{n} = \sum_{n\leq x} \frac{\chi_m(n)}{n} + \lim_{y\to\infty} \sum_{x<n\leq y} \frac{\chi_m(n)}{n},$$

Chapter 10: Dirichlet L-functions

we obtain the result

$$\sum_{n\leq x} \frac{\chi_m(n)}{n} = L_m + O\left(\frac{1}{x}\right). \tag{10.2}$$

It is possible, using a similar method to that used above, to show that the infinite series given by

$$L'_m \quad \text{and} \quad \sum_{n=1}^{\infty} \frac{\chi_m(n)}{\sqrt{n}} \tag{10.3}$$

both converge, and also that

$$\sum_{n\leq x} \frac{\chi_m(n)\log n}{n} = -L'_m + O\left(\frac{\log x}{x}\right) \tag{10.4}$$

and

$$\sum_{n\leq x} \frac{\chi_m(n)}{\sqrt{n}} = \sum_{n=1}^{\infty} \frac{\chi_m(n)}{\sqrt{n}} + O\left(\frac{1}{\sqrt{x}}\right). \tag{10.5}$$

These are all results that shall be needed in due course.

Challenge 10.3 See if you can demonstrate the convergence of L'_m by adapting the methods we used to show that L_m converges. Then go on to prove (10.4) and (10.5).

Exercise 10

1. (a) Obtain the non-principal Dirichlet character χ_2 of the group $(R_3, \otimes_3)$.
   (b) Investigate, with a piece of mathematical software or otherwise, the sum of the series

   $$L_2 = \sum_{n=1}^{\infty} \frac{\chi_2(n)}{n}.$$

   The sum is given at the back of the book, but see if you can work it out yourself before being tempted to look up the answer.

2. (a) Obtain the nth term of the sequence

$$\frac{12}{5}, \frac{72}{25}, \frac{372}{125}, \frac{1872}{625}, \ldots$$

(b) Hence, using the Cauchy convergence criterion, show that this sequence converges.

3. (a) Find the three non-principal Dirichlet characters of the group $(R_5, \otimes_5)$; you will find that two of these characters are complex-valued.

(b) Evaluate the L-functions, L_2, L_3 and L_4, associated with each of these non-principal characters. It might be easiest first to split these series into real and imaginary parts.

Chapter 11

The Möbius and Mangoldt functions

We first introduce an arithmetic function called the Möbius function, which will be needed in chapter 16. For those who have never encountered this function before, the definition may appear rather strange, maybe even a little contrived. It does, however, possess a particularly useful property that will be derived in this chapter and subsequently used to obtain a result needed in the proof of Dirichlet's theorem.

Definition 11.1 *The Möbius function μ is defined by*

$$\mu(n) = \begin{cases} 1 & \text{if } n = 1 \\ 0 & \text{if } p^2 \mid n \text{ for some prime } p \\ (-1)^k & \text{if } n = p_1 p_2 \cdots p_k, \text{ where } p_i \text{ are distinct primes.} \end{cases}$$

For example $\mu(18) = \mu(2 \times 3^2) = 0$ and $\mu(30) = \mu(2 \times 3 \times 5) = (-1)^3 = -1$. Note that from the definition of μ, $\mu(n) = 0$ if, and only if, n is divisible by a square number greater than 1.

Challenge 11.1 Prove that the Möbius function is multiplicative.

Let us first consider the sum

$$\sum_{d \mid n} \mu(d).$$

The notation indicates that this is to be taken over all factors of n. Obviously $\sum_{d|n} \mu(d) = 1$ when $n = 1$, but what about when $n > 1$? Here are two examples:

$$\sum_{d|20} \mu(d) = \mu(1) + \mu(2) + \mu(4) + \mu(5) + \mu(10) + \mu(20)$$
$$= \mu(1) + \mu(2) + \mu(2^2) + \mu(5) + \mu(2 \times 5) + \mu(2^2 \times 5)$$
$$= 1 + (-1) + 0 + (-1) + (-1)^2 + 0$$
$$= 0$$

and

$$\sum_{d|21} \mu(d) = \mu(1) + \mu(3) + \mu(7) + \mu(21)$$
$$= \mu(1) + \mu(3) + \mu(7) + \mu(3 \times 7)$$
$$= 1 + (-1) + (-1) + (-1)^2$$
$$= 0.$$

Is this a coincidence? Well, for $n > 1$, the only non-zero terms of $\sum_{d|n} \mu(d)$ will occur when d is either 1 or a product of distinct prime factors of n. So say that n has k distinct prime factors. There are $\binom{k}{m}$ possible combinations of m distinct prime factors of n. Therefore

$$\sum_{d|n} \mu(d) = \binom{k}{0}(-1)^0 + \binom{k}{1}(-1)^1 + \binom{k}{2}(-1)^2 + \ldots + \binom{k}{k}(-1)^k$$
$$= (1 + (-1))^k$$
$$= 0,$$

on using the binomial theorem. So the fact that both our examples evaluated to 0 was not a coincidence, and we have the general result

$$\sum_{d|n} \mu(d) = \begin{cases} 1 & \text{if } n = 1 \\ 0 & \text{if } n > 1. \end{cases} \qquad (11.1)$$

Associated with this sum function is something that is going to be of use later on, called the *Möbius inversion formula*. If $f(n)$ is some arithmetic function and F is defined by

$$F(n) = \sum_{d|n} f(d),$$

Chapter 11: The Möbius and Mangoldt functions

then the Möbius inversion formula provides a way of expressing f in terms of F, as follows:

$$f(n) = \sum_{d|n} \mu(d) F\left(\frac{n}{d}\right). \quad (11.2)$$

This is actually quite simple to prove, but let us first pick apart what the sum on the right-hand side of result (11.2) actually means. Since it is taken over all factors of n, and $d \times \frac{n}{d} = n$, it can be seen that the sum contains all possible expressions of the form $\mu(a)F(b)$ such that $a \times b = n$. Thus, for example,

$$\sum_{d|15} \mu(d) F\left(\frac{n}{d}\right) = \mu(1)F(15) + \mu(3)F(5) + \mu(5)F(3) + \mu(15)F(1).$$

In order to prove result (11.2), it follows, on using the definition of F, that

$$\sum_{d|n} \mu(d) F\left(\frac{n}{d}\right) = \sum_{d|n} \mu(d) \left(\sum_{k|\frac{n}{d}} f(k) \right)$$
$$= \sum_{d|n} \sum_{k|\frac{n}{d}} \mu(d) f(k).$$

This double sum might look a little intimidating at first, but it just represents the sum of all possible products $\mu(d)f(k)$ such that d is a factor of n and k is a factor of $\frac{n}{d}$; see appendix E for an introduction to double sums. For example,

$$\sum_{d|15} \sum_{k|\frac{15}{d}} \mu(d) f(k) = \mu(1)\{f(1) + f(3) + f(5) + f(15)\}$$
$$+ \mu(3)\{f(1) + f(5)\}$$
$$+ \mu(5)\{f(1) + f(3)\} + \mu(15)f(1).$$

Now, since $d \mid n$ and $k \mid \frac{n}{d}$ if, and only if, $k \mid n$ and $d \mid \frac{n}{k}$ (see challenge 11.2), it is the case that

$$\sum_{d|n} \sum_{k|\frac{n}{d}} \mu(d) f(k) = \sum_{k|n} \sum_{d|\frac{n}{k}} \mu(d) f(k)$$
$$= \sum_{k|n} f(k) \sum_{d|\frac{n}{k}} \mu(d)$$

$$= \sum_{k=n} f(k)$$
$$= f(n).$$

To obtain the third line it simply needs to be noted, from result (11.1), that $\sum_{d \mid \frac{n}{k}} \mu(d) = 0$ unless $\frac{n}{k} = 1$ (that is, $k = n$), in which case the sum is equal to 1.

Challenge 11.2 Rather than take it on trust, prove the claim made above that $d \mid n$ and $k \mid \frac{n}{d}$ if, and only if, $k \mid n$ and $d \mid \frac{n}{k}$.

We next demonstrate an application of the Möbius inversion formula to obtain a result that will be needed in due course. This result concerns the following function.

Definition 11.2 *The* Mangoldt function, *denoted by Λ, is an arithmetic function defined as follows:*

$$\Lambda(n) = \begin{cases} \log p & \text{if } n = p^k \text{ for some prime } p \text{ and } k \in \mathbb{N} \\ 0 & \text{otherwise.} \end{cases}$$

In other words, $\Lambda(n)$ is only non-zero when n is a power of a prime, and in that case it is equal to the natural logarithm of that prime. Note that this is the type of conditional definition of an arithmetic function referred to in chapter 4. Table 11.1 evaluates $\Lambda(n)$ from $n = 1$ to $n = 10$:

Let us show first that

$$\sum_{d \mid n} \Lambda(d) = \log n. \tag{11.3}$$

A formal symbolic proof could be provided here, but this would mask the simplicity of what is actually going on. To convince ourselves that this result is actually true, we just need to note that, for a particular prime p appearing in the prime factorisation of n, a term $\log p$ will appear in the sum on the right for every d that is a power of p, but will not appear for any other values of d. Thus the number of times $\log p$ appears in total will be equal to the power of p in the prime factorisation of n. On applying this argument to all the other prime factors of n, we get our result by a simple application of the laws of logarithms.

Chapter 11: The Möbius and Mangoldt functions

n	$\Lambda(n)$
1	0
2	$\log 2$
3	$\log 3$
4	$\log 2$
5	$\log 5$
6	0
7	$\log 7$
8	$\log 2$
9	$\log 3$
10	0

Table 11.1

By way of an illustrative example, consider the situation for $n = 40$:

$$\begin{aligned}\sum_{d|40} \Lambda(d) &= \Lambda(1) + \Lambda(2) + \Lambda(4) + \Lambda(5) + \Lambda(8) + \Lambda(10) + \Lambda(20) + \Lambda(40) \\ &= \Lambda(1) + \Lambda(2) + \Lambda(2^2) + \Lambda(5) + \Lambda(2^3) \\ &\quad + \Lambda(2 \times 5) + \Lambda(2^2 \times 5) + \Lambda(2^3 \times 5) \\ &= 0 + \log 2 + \log 2 + \log 5 + \log 2 + 0 + 0 + 0 \\ &= \log(2^3 \times 5) \\ &= \log 40.\end{aligned}$$

Notice, once more, how the Fundamental Theorem of Arithmetic is inextricably linked in with definitions of, and hence calculations associated with, arithmetic functions.

From result (11.3) it follows, on putting $f(n) = \Lambda(n)$ and $F(n) = \log n$ in result (11.2), that

$$\Lambda(n) = \sum_{d|n} \mu(d) \log\left(\frac{n}{d}\right), \qquad (11.4)$$

a result that will be exploited in chapter 16. To illustrate this, recall, from definition 11.2 that $\Lambda(9) = \log 3$ and $\Lambda(10) = 0$. The right-hand side of result (11.4) in each case is given by

$$\begin{aligned}\sum_{d|9} \mu(d) \log\left(\frac{9}{d}\right) &= \mu(1) \log 9 + \mu(3) \log 3 + \mu(9) \log 1 \\ &= 1 \times \log 9 + (-1) \log 3 + 0 \times 0\end{aligned}$$

$$= \log 9 - \log 3$$
$$= \log 3$$

and

$$\sum_{d|10} \mu(d) \log\left(\frac{10}{d}\right) = \mu(1)\log 10 + \mu(2)\log 5 + \mu(5)\log 2 + \mu(10)\log 1$$
$$= 1 \times \log 10 + (-1)\log 5 + (-1)\log 2 + (-1)^2 \times 0$$
$$= \log 10 - \log 5 - \log 2$$
$$= 0,$$

respectively.

We now define a mathematical symbol that will be used both in this and in forthcoming chapters:

Definition 11.3 *The symbol $\lfloor \ \rfloor$ denotes the floor function, with $\lfloor x \rfloor$ being the greatest integer less than or equal to x.*

Here are some examples to help clarify this definition:

$$\lfloor 5\tfrac{1}{4} \rfloor = 5, \quad \lfloor 8 \rfloor = 8, \quad \lfloor \pi \rfloor = 3 \quad \text{and} \quad \lfloor -5\tfrac{1}{4} \rfloor = -6.$$

In other words, the floor function rounds numbers down.

Finally in this chapter we obtain two further results concerning the Mangoldt function. The first of these is

$$\sum_{n \leq x} \Lambda(n) \left\lfloor \frac{x}{n} \right\rfloor = \sum_{n \leq x} \sum_{d|n} \Lambda(d) \qquad (11.5)$$

As with the double sums we met earlier, this might seem a little daunting initially. For the sake of clarity, therefore, we will briefly illustrate, by way of an example, the meaning of the expression on the right-hand side of result (11.5). Let us evaluate this for $x = 4\tfrac{1}{3}$. When $n = 1$ on the outer sum, the inner sum just gives rise to $\Lambda(1)$ because 1 is the only factor of 1. Since 1 and 2 are the factors of 2, the inner sum contributes $\Lambda(1) + \Lambda(2)$ when $n = 2$ on the outer sum. Similarly, the inner sum gives $\Lambda(1) + \Lambda(3)$ and $\Lambda(1) + \Lambda(2) + \Lambda(4)$ for $n = 3$ and $n = 4$, respectively, on the outer sum. It is therefore the case that

$$\sum_{n \leq 4\tfrac{1}{3}} \sum_{d|n} \Lambda(d) = \{\Lambda(1)\} + \{\Lambda(1) + \Lambda(2)\} + \{\Lambda(1) + \Lambda(3)\}$$
$$+ \{\Lambda(1) + \Lambda(2) + \Lambda(4)\}$$
$$= 4\Lambda(1) + 2\Lambda(2) + \Lambda(3) + \Lambda(4)$$
$$= 3\log 2 + \log 3,$$

on utilising the definition of the Mangoldt function.

To see that result (11.5) is in fact true, it may be noted that both sides are just summing the same things in a different order. For example, with $x = 4\frac{1}{3}$ once more, let us count the total number of appearances of the term $\Lambda(2)$ on the right-hand side. We see that, for a particular value of $n \leq 4\frac{1}{3}$ on the outer sum, exactly one $\Lambda(2)$ appears on the inner sum if, and only if, 2 divides n. Therefore the only contributions to $\Lambda(2)$ occur when $n = 2$ and $n = 4$, giving $2\Lambda(2)$. On the other hand, the expression $\lfloor \frac{x}{2} \rfloor = 2$ counts the number of integers n in the set $\{n : 1 \leq n \leq 4\frac{1}{3}\}$ that are divisible by 2. This gives rise to the term $\Lambda(2)\lfloor \frac{x}{2} \rfloor = 2\Lambda(2)$ appearing on the left-hand side. It is easy to generalise this argument to obtain result (11.5).

Our last result here follows easily from results (11.3) and (11.5):

$$\sum_{n \leq x} \Lambda(n) \left\lfloor \frac{x}{n} \right\rfloor = \sum_{n \leq x} \sum_{d \mid n} \Lambda(d)$$
$$= \sum_{n \leq x} \log n. \qquad (11.6)$$

Exercise 11

1. Evaluate each of the following:
   (a) $\mu(98)$;
   (b) $\mu(286)$;
   (c) $\mu(5!)$.

2. Find, with justification, all values of $n \in \mathbb{N}$ for which $\mu(n!) \neq 0$.

3. Evaluate each of the following, expressing your answers as single logarithms:
   (a) $\sum_{k=8}^{15} \Lambda(k)$;
   (b) $\sum_{d \mid 15} \Lambda(d)$;
   (c) $\sum_{d \mid 6} d\Lambda(d)$.

4. State, with justification, whether or not the Mangoldt function is multiplicative.

5. Calculate the value of each of these numerical expressions involving the floor function:
   (a) $\lfloor 2\sqrt{7} \rfloor + \lfloor 3\sqrt{7} \rfloor$;
   (b) $\lfloor 2\sqrt{7} + 3\sqrt{7} \rfloor$;
   (c) $\sum_{n \leq 6\pi} \left\lfloor \dfrac{6\pi}{n} \right\rfloor$.

6. Find the smallest possible value of x for which
$$\sum_{n \leq x} \Lambda(n) \left\lfloor \frac{x}{n} \right\rfloor > 10.$$

7. Let $n \in \mathbb{N}$.
   (a) Find the possible values of $\mu(n(n+1))$ and $\mu(n(n+2))$.
   (b) Show that $\mu(n)\mu(n+1)\mu(n+2)\mu(n+3) = 0$.

8. Give the values of $\Lambda(n!)$ for $n = 1, 2, 3, \ldots$.

9. In challenge 11.1 you were asked to show that the Möbius function is multiplicative. Show, by way of a counterexample, that it is not completely multiplicative.

10. Consider the arithmetic functions $\tau(n)$ and $\sigma(n)$ studied in chapter 4.
    (a) Use the Möbius inversion formula to show that
$$\sum_{d|n} \mu\left(\frac{n}{d}\right) \tau(d) = 1 \quad \text{and} \quad \sum_{d|n} \mu\left(\frac{n}{d}\right) \sigma(d) = n.$$
    (b) Illustrate each of these formulae with an example.

11. Prove that
$$\sum_{d^2 | n} \mu(d) = \{\mu(n)\}^2.$$

Chapter 12

The generalised Möbius inversion formula

If any of the chapters in this book are suitable for bedtime reading then this probably will not be one of them! The work here is rather technical, but please be patient; it might take several sittings before you are really happy with what is going on, although this will be time well spent. An understanding of the ideas and results presented here is essential in order to be able to follow certain parts of our proof of Dirichlet's theorem. Before quoting the generalised Möbius inversion formula and then showing that it is true, some key concepts are developed.

Definition 12.1 *The* Dirichlet product *(also known as* Dirichlet convolution*) of two arithmetic functions, f and g, is defined to be the arithmetic function h given by*

$$h(n) = \sum_{d|n} f(d) g\left(\frac{n}{d}\right).$$

This is also written as $(f * g)(n)$.

It is worth noting that $(f * g)(n) = (g * f)(n)$, which follows since the set consisting of all possible ordered pairs $(d, \frac{n}{d})$ is the same as that comprising all possible ordered pairs $(\frac{n}{d}, d)$.

Definition 12.1 probably reminds you of the Möbius inversion formula (11.2). In fact, some might initially be slightly thrown by the use of the word 'product' here since it is usually associated with multiplication in arithmetic. However, in higher mathematics, the word 'product' has a more general meaning, and is often referred to as a binary operation. In other words, a product might be regarded as an operation for which there are two inputs and one output. Recall that binary operations were discussed in connection with groups in chapter 6. For the particular case of the Dirichlet product, the two inputs and the output are each arithmetic functions.

To take an example, we will show that

$$\phi(n) = \sum_{d|n} \mu(d)\frac{n}{d},$$

which says that Euler's phi-function is the Dirichlet product of the Möbius function $f(n) = \mu(n)$ and the function $g(n) = n$. It might be an idea to remind yourself about the definition and properties of $\phi(n)$ before going any further; refer back to chapter 4. The following intermediate result is striking because of the beautiful simplicity of its statement.

Lemma 12.2

$$\sum_{d|n} \phi(d) = n.$$

PROOF The integers in the set $S = \{1, 2, 3, \ldots, n\}$ are split up into k subsets, where k is the number of factors of n. Each subset corresponds to a particular factor of n. The subset corresponding to the factor d of n consists of all integers $m \in S$ for which $\gcd(m, n) = d$. Notice that each element of S will lie in exactly one of the subsets.

Since $\gcd(m, n) = d$, if, and only if $\gcd(\frac{m}{d}, \frac{n}{d}) = 1$, the number of integers in the subset corresponding to d is equal to $\phi(\frac{n}{d})$. Then, on summing over all the factors of d, we obtain

$$\sum_{d|n} \phi\left(\frac{n}{d}\right) = n.$$

The result follows, on noting that

$$\sum_{d|n} \phi\left(\frac{n}{d}\right) = \sum_{d|n} \phi(d)$$

since the sum on the left runs through all the factors of n backwards from n to 1, and the sum on the left runs through them forwards from 1 to n. □

Chapter 12: The generalised Möbius inversion formula

To illustrate lemma 12.2,

$$\sum_{d|18} \phi(d) = \phi(1) + \phi(2) + \phi(3) + \phi(6) + \phi(9) + \phi(18)$$
$$= 1 + 1 + 2 + 2 + 6 + 6$$
$$= 18.$$

Theorem 12.3

$$\phi(n) = \sum_{d|n} \mu(d) \frac{n}{d},$$

or, in other words, the Dirichlet product of $\mu(n)$ and n is $\phi(n)$.

PROOF Let

$$F(n) = \sum_{d|n} \phi(d).$$

Then, using the Möbius inversion formula (11.2) with $f(n) = \phi(n)$, we obtain

$$\phi(n) = \sum_{d|n} \mu(d) F\left(\frac{n}{d}\right).$$

However, from lemma 12.2, we know that $F(n) = n$. This is enough to prove the theorem. □

Challenge 12.1 Suppose that f and g are multiplicative arithmetic functions. Prove that $f * g$, their Dirichlet product, is also multiplicative. This is quite a tough challenge, but do not be tempted to look at the back of the book too soon. You can return to it later, as this result is not used in our proof of Dirichlet's theorem.

It is appropriate, at this point, to introduce yet another arithmetic function:

Definition 12.4 *The arithmetic function $I(n)$ is defined to be 1 when $n = 1$ and 0 when $n > 1$.*

This function behaves, with regard to Dirichlet multiplication, just like the number 1 does in normal multiplication of numbers since

$$(f * I)(n) = \sum_{d|n} f(d) I\left(\frac{n}{d}\right)$$
$$= f(n)$$

for all positive integers n. This is because $I(\frac{n}{d}) = 1$ when $d = n$ but $I(\frac{n}{d}) = 0$ otherwise. It is possible to obtain, similarly, the result $(I * f)(n) = f(n)$.

So we have defined a binary operation on arithmetic functions, and discovered that there is an element that acts as an identity with respect to this binary operation. An obvious question is, therefore, does there exist a unique function f^{-1} such that

$$(f^{-1} * f)(n) = (f * f^{-1})(n) = I(n)$$

for all positive integers n? In other words, do we have inverses? The answer is, as shall be seen, in the affirmative so long as $f(1) \neq 0$. Note that, since $(f * g)(n) = (g * f)(n)$, we only need to check that $(f^{-1} * f)(n) = I(n)$.

We can use an inductive argument to find the values of $f^{-1}(n)$, $n = 1, 2, 3, \ldots$, in a recursive manner. When $n = 1$ the equation simplifies to $f^{-1}(1)f(1) = I(1) = 1$, giving

$$f^{-1}(1) = \frac{1}{f(1)},$$

and showing why the condition $f(1) \neq 0$ is necessary. Now assume that $f^{-1}(n)$ is uniquely determined for all n such that $n \leq k$ for some positive integer k. We need to solve the equation $(f^{-1} * f)(k+1) = I(k+1)$, which we may rewrite as

$$\sum_{d|(k+1)} f^{-1}(d) f\left(\frac{k+1}{d}\right) = 0,$$

or, on writing the last term in the sum separately, as

$$f^{-1}(k+1)f(1) + \sum_{\substack{d|(k+1) \\ d \leq k}} f^{-1}(d) f\left(\frac{k+1}{d}\right) = 0.$$

The inductive hypothesis is then utilised to obtain the unique value

$$f^{-1}(k+1) = -\frac{1}{f(1)} \sum_{\substack{d|(k+1) \\ d \leq k}} f^{-1}(d) f\left(\frac{k+1}{d}\right), \qquad (12.1)$$

as required, noting that the condition $f(1) \neq 0$ is also needed here. We call the function f^{-1} the *Dirichlet inverse* of f.

It may be seen that result (12.1) provides a recursive method of calculating the Dirichlet inverse of any arithmetic function f. Suppose, for example, that $f(n) = \tau(n)$, the number of factors of n. Then

$$\tau^{-1}(1) = \frac{1}{\tau(1)} = 1,$$

$$\tau^{-1}(2) = -\sum_{\substack{d|2 \\ d\leq 1}} \tau^{-1}(d)\tau\left(\frac{2}{d}\right) = -\tau^{-1}(1)\tau(2) = -2,$$

$$\tau^{-1}(3) = -\sum_{\substack{d|3 \\ d\leq 2}} \tau^{-1}(d)\tau\left(\frac{3}{d}\right) = -\tau^{-1}(1)\tau(3) = -2,$$

$$\tau^{-1}(4) = -\sum_{\substack{d|4 \\ d\leq 3}} \tau^{-1}(d)\tau\left(\frac{4}{d}\right) = -\tau^{-1}(1)\tau(4) - \tau^{-1}(2)\tau(2) = 1,$$

and so on. These results are summarised and extended in table 12.1.

n	$\tau(n)$	$\tau^{-1}(n)$
1	1	1
2	2	−2
3	2	−2
4	3	1
5	2	−2
6	4	4
7	2	−2
8	4	0

Table 12.1

Mathematicians like to generalise things as much as possible, and the Dirichlet product (or convolution) can in fact be generalised somewhat, as follows. Suppose that f is still an arithmetic function but that G is some function defined on the positive real numbers; thus, for example, we would allow functions like $G(x) = \sin x$. Then the Dirichlet product may be generalised by way of:

Definition 12.5 *The* generalised convolution *of the arithmetic function f and* the arbitrary function G is defined to be the function H given by

$$H(x) = \sum_{n \leq x} f(n) G\left(\frac{x}{n}\right)$$

for any $x > 0$. This product is denoted by $(f \circ G)(x)$.

To take a simple example, let $f(n) = \tau(n)$ once more and $G(x) = 3x^2 + 2$. Then

$$H(\sqrt{12}) = \sum_{n \leq \sqrt{12}} \tau(n) \left\{ 3\left(\frac{\sqrt{12}}{n}\right)^2 + 2 \right\}$$

$$= \sum_{n \leq 3} \tau(n) \left\{ \frac{36}{n^2} + 2 \right\}$$

$$= \tau(1)\{36 + 2\} + \tau(2)\left\{\frac{36}{2^2} + 2\right\} + \tau(3)\left\{\frac{36}{3^2} + 2\right\}$$

$$= 38 + 22 + 12$$

$$= 72.$$

Note that in the case where G is a function such that $G(x) = 0$ whenever x is not an integer, it is true that $(f \circ G)(n) = (f * G)(n)$. This is why the convolution given in definition 12.5 is considered to be a generalisation of the Dirichlet product.

Research activity 12.1 Convolutions occur in other areas of mathematics, and in slightly different forms. For example, in probability theory the convolution of the probability density functions of two continuous random variables X and Y gives rise to the probability density function of $X + Y$. As an aside, you might want to investigate this further.

If α and β are any two arithmetic functions, and G is any function defined on all positive real numbers, then

$$(\alpha \circ (\beta \circ G))(x) = \sum_{n \leq x} \alpha(n)(\beta \circ G)\left(\frac{x}{n}\right)$$

$$= \sum_{n \leq x} \alpha(n) \sum_{k \leq \frac{x}{n}} \beta(k) G\left(\frac{x}{nk}\right)$$

Chapter 12: The generalised Möbius inversion formula

$$= \sum_{n \leq x} \sum_{k \leq \frac{x}{n}} \alpha(n)\beta(k)G\left(\frac{x}{nk}\right)$$

$$= \sum_{nk \leq x} \alpha(n)\beta(k)G\left(\frac{x}{nk}\right),$$

where the final sum is over all possible pairs of positive integers n and k such that $nk \leq x$, noting that the process of summing over all n and k such that $n \leq x$ and $k \leq \frac{x}{n}$ respectively is equivalent to that of summing over all n and k such that $nk \leq x$. It then follows, on letting $m = nk$, that

$$(\alpha \circ (\beta \circ G))(x) = \sum_{m \leq x} \left\{ \sum_{n|m} \alpha(n)\beta\left(\frac{m}{n}\right) \right\} G\left(\frac{x}{m}\right)$$

$$= \sum_{m \leq x} (\alpha * \beta)(m) G\left(\frac{x}{m}\right)$$

$$= ((\alpha * \beta) \circ G)(x).$$

It is also clear that

$$(I \circ G)(x) = \sum_{n \leq x} I(n) G\left(\frac{x}{n}\right)$$

$$= G(x).$$

Now say that an arithmetic function f has Dirichlet inverse f^{-1}, and that

$$H(x) = \sum_{n \leq x} f(n) G\left(\frac{x}{n}\right)$$

$$= (f \circ G)(x).$$

Then, on using the above results, we have

$$f^{-1} \circ H = f^{-1} \circ (f \circ G)$$
$$= (f^{-1} * f) \circ G$$
$$= I \circ G$$
$$= G,$$

which shows that

$$G(x) = \sum_{n \leq x} f^{-1}(n) H\left(\frac{x}{n}\right).$$

Challenge 12.2 In a similar manner, obtain the result

$$G(x) = \sum_{n \leq x} f^{-1}(n) H\left(\frac{x}{n}\right) \Rightarrow H(x) = \sum_{n \leq x} f(n) G\left(\frac{x}{n}\right).$$

From the above it follows that

$$H(x) = \sum_{n \leq x} f(n) G\left(\frac{x}{n}\right) \Leftrightarrow G(x) = \sum_{n \leq x} f^{-1}(n) H\left(\frac{x}{n}\right). \quad (12.2)$$

We are now able to state the *generalised Möbius inversion formula* since it is related to result (12.2). It tells us that if α is a completely multiplicative arithmetic function such that α is not identically zero (see chapter 4 for a reminder of what "completely multiplicative" means) then

$$G(x) = \sum_{n \leq x} \alpha(n) F\left(\frac{x}{n}\right) \Leftrightarrow F(x) = \sum_{n \leq x} \mu(n) \alpha(n) G\left(\frac{x}{n}\right). \quad (12.3)$$

All that needs to be done in order to demonstrate the truth of result (12.3) is to prove that if α is completely multiplicative then $\alpha^{-1}(n) = \mu(n)\alpha(n)$ for all positive integers n. So say that α is a completely multiplicative arithmetic function. Then, with $g(n) = \mu(n)\alpha(n)$, it follows that

$$(g * \alpha)(n) = \sum_{d|n} \mu(d)\alpha(d)\alpha\left(\frac{n}{d}\right)$$

$$= \sum_{d|n} \mu(d)\alpha\left(d \cdot \frac{n}{d}\right)$$

$$= \alpha(n) \sum_{d|n} \mu(d)$$

$$= \alpha(n) I(n)$$

$$= I(n),$$

showing that $\alpha^{-1}(n) = g(n) = \mu(n)\alpha(n)$. Just in case you are wondering about the last couple of steps in the above calculation, result (11.1) on page 84 gives

$$\sum_{d|n} \mu(n) = I(n),$$

and it is also true, as a consequence of α being a multiplicative arithmetic function, that $\alpha(1) = 1$ so long as α is not identically zero; see challenge 4.2

on page 29. Thus, assuming that α is completely multiplicative, we may put $f = \alpha$ in result (12.2) to obtain result (12.3), the generalised Möbius inversion formula.

Challenge 12.3 Show how the ordinary Möbius inversion formula (11.2) follows from result (12.3).

Exercise 12

1. Let f be the Dirichlet product of Euler's phi function and the sum-of-factors function, denoted by of ϕ and σ, respectively. Calculate $f(6)$.

2. With the help of result (12.1), tabulate the values of $\sigma^{-1}(n)$, the Dirichet inverse of $\sigma(n)$, from $n = 1$ to $n = 8$.

3. From challenge 12.1 we know that $f * g$ is multiplicative if both f and g are multiplicative. Show that it is not necessarily the case that $f * g$ is completely multiplicative whenever f and g are both completely multiplicative.

4. Calculate $(f \circ G)(\pi)$, where $f(n) = \sigma(n)$ and $G(x) = \cos x$.

5. Let $f(n) = 2n$ and $G(x) = x + 1$. Obtain a simplified expression for $(f \circ G)(x)$, the generalised convolution of f and G.

6. (a) Calculate both
$$\phi^{-1}(n) \quad \text{and} \quad \sum_{d|n} d\mu(d)$$
for $n = 1$ to $n = 6$.
   (b) Make a conjecture based on your numerical evidence, and attempt to prove it.

Part III

The proof

Chapter 13

The road map

The purpose of this chapter is to indicate how the proof of Dirichlet's theorem will proceed, without getting overly technical about it. The hope is that this will enable the reader to keep in mind the 'big picture' of the proof whilst navigating through some new and relatively difficult mathematics. It might be worth revisiting this chapter every now and again in order fully to appreciate the structural aspects.

We start by explaining the fundamental idea behind the proof. Remember that our ultimate goal is to show that, for any $a, b \in \mathbb{N}$, the arithmetic sequence
$$b, a+b, 2a+b, 3a+b, \ldots \tag{13.1}$$
contains infinitely primes provided that $\gcd(a,b) = 1$. It is certainly very easy to prove special cases of this theorem. For example, in chapter 1 we saw just how straightforward it is, using Euclid's proof, to show that there are infinitely many prime numbers; this covers the case $a = 2, b = 1$. There would, however, appear to be no correspondingly simple way to prove the general result.

In our search for an alternative way into this problem, let us cast our minds back to chapter 3, in which we derived the result
$$\sum_{k=1}^{n} \frac{1}{p_k} \to \infty \quad \text{as} \quad n \to \infty,$$
where p_k denotes the kth prime. Note that, although it might not be regarded as the most efficient of approaches, this does provide us with

another proof of the infinitude of the primes. Dirichlet was in fact able successfully to prove his theorem by adapting this idea. He considered the function
$$F(x) = \sum_{n \leq x} f(n),$$
where
$$f(n) = \begin{cases} \frac{1}{n} & \text{if } n \text{ both belongs to the sequence (13.1) and is prime} \\ 0 & \text{otherwise.} \end{cases}$$

For example, $a = 5$, $b = 2$, then
$$F(25\tfrac{2}{3}) = \sum_{n \leq 25\frac{2}{3}} f(n)$$
$$= \sum_{n=1}^{25} f(n)$$
$$= f(2) + f(7) + f(12) + f(17) + f(22)$$
$$= \frac{1}{2} + \frac{1}{7} + 0 + \frac{1}{17} + 0$$
$$= \frac{167}{238}.$$

A more concise way of writing $F(x)$ is as
$$\sum_{\substack{p \leq x \\ p \equiv b \pmod{a}}} \frac{1}{p},$$

where the notation indicates that the sum is to be taken over all primes p no greater than $x \in \mathbb{R}$ such that p satisfies $p \equiv b \pmod{a}$; note that $p \equiv b \pmod{a}$ if, and only if, $p = an + b$ for some $n \geq 0$.

Dirichlet managed to show that $F(x) \to \infty$ as $x \to \infty$ [9], thereby proving the theorem. His proof, however, was analytic. In order to understand it, one requires a degree of expertise in certain areas of complex analysis. It turns out though that it is possible to obtain an elementary proof of Dirichlet's theorem by studying the similar-looking sum

$$\sum_{\substack{p \leq x \\ p \equiv b \pmod{a}}} \frac{\log p}{p}. \qquad (13.2)$$

Chapter 13: The road map 105

This is the approach adopted by Shapiro [18], and indeed the one we will be following in this book. If the sum (13.2) can be shown to tend to infinity as x does, then Dirichlet's theorem will have been proved. This is far from easy to do, however, and we will need to work towards this result in stages.

We want to avoid getting too bogged down with unnecessary mathematical detail at this point, but it is important, before embarking on the proof proper, to have at least some idea of how the concepts and techniques covered in the Toolkit will be utilised in the coming chapters. This will indeed be crucial with regard to obtaining an initial understanding of the various key ideas that emerge as we make our way through the proof.

The first step will be to show that

$$\sum_{p \leq x} \frac{\log p}{p} = \log x + O(1), \qquad (13.3)$$

where the sum is taken over all primes p less than $x \in \mathbb{R}$. This says that the sum on the left-hand side behaves rather like $\log x$ for large x; note the use of 'big oh' notation here. It does actually require some effort to prove this result, although the underlying mathematics is certainly not too intimidating. We will make of use the Mangoldt function, introduced in chapter 11, taking advantage of its properties in order to be able to estimate various associated sums using integrals. The sole purpose of chapter 14 is to prove result (13.3).

Of course, a problem with result (13.3) as it stands is that the sum is over *all* primes less than x rather than just those appearing in $\{an + b : n \geq 0\}$. We thus need some way of picking out just the primes in the arithmetic progression, and seek a mathematical tool that can be used to extract all the relevant terms from result (13.3) while still retaining some information on how their sum grows as x increases. In fact, 'extract' is a nice word to use here since, making an analogy with dentistry, we would like to possess a tool to perform this extraction as simply and painlessly as possible. This is where the Dirichlet characters come in; their orthogonality properties happen to be ideal for this task.

There is, however, a further complication. Although we may use the characters to obtain an expression for result (13.2), this expression has a 'nice part',

$$\frac{1}{\phi(a)} \log x, \qquad (13.4)$$

and a 'horrible part',

$$\frac{1}{\phi(a)} \sum_{m=2}^{\phi(a)} \overline{\chi}_m(b) \sum_{p \leq x} \frac{\chi_m(p) \log p}{p} + O(1). \tag{13.5}$$

Do not be too concerned about the rather unpleasant-looking expression (13.5); all will be explained in chapter 15. It is clear, on considering these two parts, that if it could be proved that (13.5) is bounded then we would have finished, since this would imply that the sum of (13.4) and (13.5) tends to infinity as x does. In order to show that (13.5) is indeed bounded, it suffices, as will be proved in chapter 15, to demonstrate that

$$\sum_{p \leq x} \frac{\chi_m(p) \log p}{p} = O(1) \tag{13.6}$$

for each non-principal Dirichlet character $\chi_2, \chi_3, \ldots, \chi_{\phi(a)}$.

It turns out that there is not much we can do with the left-hand side of result (13.6) as it stands, so the next step will be to transform it into the more amenable sum

$$-L'_m \sum_{n \leq x} \frac{\mu(n) \chi_m(n)}{n} + O(1) \tag{13.7}$$

involving the Möbius function and Dirichlet L-functions. (Note that the sum is over all positive integers not exceeding x rather than just over the primes.) This will be carried out in chapter 16. Then, remembering from chapter 10 that L'_m converges for all non-principal characters, we see that all there is left to do is to show that

$$\sum_{n \leq x} \frac{\mu(n) \chi_m(n)}{n} = O(1) \tag{13.8}$$

for each non-principal character.

In chapter 17 the related result

$$L_m \sum_{n \leq x} \frac{\mu(n) \chi_m(n)}{n} = O(1). \tag{13.9}$$

is obtained by using the generalised Möbius inversion formula. Note that this would imply the truth of result (13.8) provided that $L_m \neq 0$ for each non-principal character. This is proved to be the case for all real-valued characters in chapter 17, which turns out to be a rather technical piece of work.

The final part of the proof, given in chapter 18, involves verifing that $L_m \neq 0$ for all complex-valued characters. This is proved by contradiction, where further use is made of the generalised Möbius inversion formula.

Chapter 14

Estimating some sums

In this chapter we focus on the estimation of several sums. In particular, we prove that

$$\sum_{p \leq x} \frac{\log p}{p} = \log x + O(1), \qquad (14.1)$$

where the condition on the sum indicates that it is to be taken over all primes p not greater than x. So, for example,

$$\sum_{p \leq 4\pi} \frac{\log p}{p} = \frac{\log 2}{2} + \frac{\log 3}{3} + \frac{\log 5}{5} + \frac{\log 7}{7} + \frac{\log 11}{11}.$$

It will be assumed, in what follows, that $x \in \mathbb{R}$ and $x \geq 2$. Result (14.1) is another example of an asymptotic relation; we have already met some of these in chapters 5, 10 and 13. As a point of interest, note that it implies, as a consequence of the fact that $\log x \to \infty$ as $x \to \infty$, that there are infinitely prime numbers.

The proof of result (14.1) is not an entirely straightforward matter, and will require several steps. We show first that

$$\sum_{n \leq x} \log n = x \log x - x + O(\log x), \qquad (14.2)$$

which, in conjunction with result (11.6) on page 89, implies that

$$\sum_{n \leq x} \Lambda(n) \left\lfloor \frac{x}{n} \right\rfloor = x \log x - x + O(\log x). \qquad (14.3)$$

The next step is to prove that

$$\sum_{p \leq x} \left\lfloor \frac{x}{p} \right\rfloor \log p = x \log x + O(x). \qquad (14.4)$$

With a little bit of effort this does eventually lead to result (14.1). The proofs of these results will involve the use of integrals to approximate certain sums, and also manipulations both of the floor function and of various series.

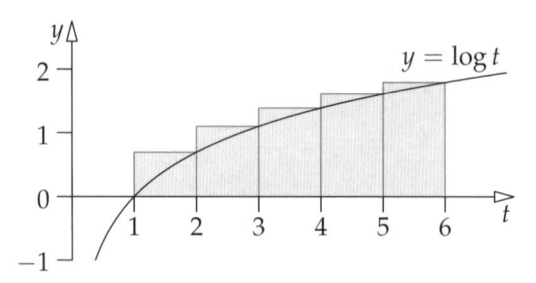

Figure 14.1

The proof of result (14.2) is in fact very straightforward. By considering both the area under the curve $y = \log t$ from $t = 1$ to $t = 6$ and the combined area of the five rectangles in figure 14.1, we see that

$$\int_1^6 \log t \, dt < \sum_{n=2}^6 \log n = \sum_{n=1}^6 \log n.$$

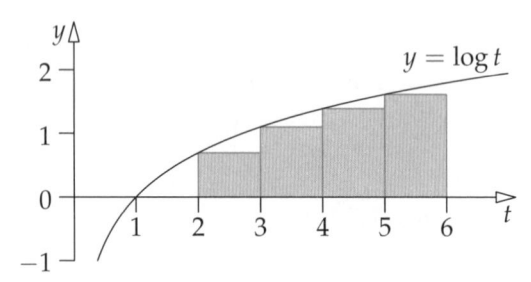

Figure 14.2

Similarly, from figure 14.2, it follows that

$$\sum_{n=1}^5 \log n < \int_1^6 \log t \, dt.$$

Chapter 14: Estimating some sums 111

Combining these inequalities gives

$$\sum_{n=1}^{5} \log n < \int_{1}^{6} \log t \, dt < \sum_{n=2}^{6} \log n = \sum_{n=1}^{6} \log n,$$

which is depicted in figure 14.3.

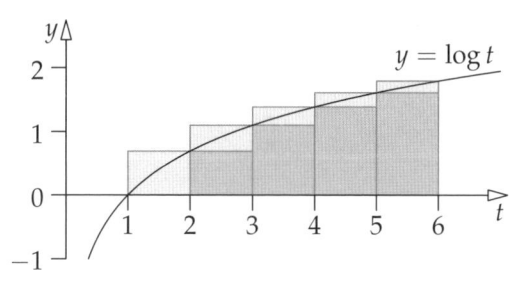

Figure 14.3

By extending and generalising this idea it can be seen that the following chain of inequalities will, for any $x \in \mathbb{R}$ such that $x \geq 2$, certainly always hold:

$$\sum_{n=1}^{\lfloor x \rfloor - 1} \log n < \int_{1}^{x} \log t \, dt < \sum_{n=1}^{\lfloor x \rfloor + 1} \log n, \tag{14.5}$$

noting the use of the dummy variable t in the integral.

Challenge 14.1 By drawing diagrams similar to those in figures 14.1 and 14.2, satisfy yourself that result (14.5) is actually true. Remember that we are not assuming that x is an integer.

Since

$$\sum_{n=1}^{\lfloor x \rfloor - 1} \log n = \sum_{n \leq x} \log n - \log \lfloor x \rfloor$$

and

$$\sum_{n=1}^{\lfloor x \rfloor + 1} \log n = \sum_{n \leq x} \log n + \log(\lfloor x \rfloor + 1),$$

it follows from result (14.5) that

$$\sum_{n \leq x} \log n - \log \lfloor x \rfloor < x \log x - x + 1 < \sum_{n \leq x} \log n + \log(\lfloor x \rfloor + 1).$$

On rearrangement, this gives

$$x \log x - x + 1 - \log(\lfloor x \rfloor + 1) < \sum_{n \leq x} \log n < x \log x - x + 1 + \log \lfloor x \rfloor.$$
(14.6)

Then, as $2x \geq \lfloor x \rfloor + x \geq \lfloor x \rfloor + 1$ for $x \geq 1$, and $\log x$ is an increasing function, result (14.6) gives

$$x \log x - x - \log 2x + 1 < \sum_{n \leq x} \log n < x \log x - x + 1 + \log x$$

for $x \geq 2$. Translating this into the 'big oh' notation leads to result (14.2):

$$\sum_{n \leq x} \log n = x \log x - x + O(\log x),$$

from which we obtain, on using result (11.6) on page 89, result (14.3):

$$\sum_{n \leq x} \Lambda(n) \left\lfloor \frac{x}{n} \right\rfloor = x \log x - x + O(\log x).$$

The goal of this chapter, that of proving result (14.1), is getting ever closer, and the next step is to use result (14.3) to help prove result (14.4):

$$\sum_{p \leq x} \left\lfloor \frac{x}{p} \right\rfloor \log p = x \log x + O(x),$$

where, as the notation indicates, the sum is extended over all primes less than or equal to x.

Recalling that $\Lambda(n) = 0$ unless n is a power of a prime, we obtain

$$\sum_{n \leq x} \Lambda(n) \left\lfloor \frac{x}{n} \right\rfloor = \sum_{p \leq x} \sum_{k=1}^{\infty} \Lambda(p^k) \left\lfloor \frac{x}{p^k} \right\rfloor$$

$$= \sum_{p \leq x} \left\lfloor \frac{x}{p} \right\rfloor \log p + \sum_{p \leq x} \log p \sum_{k=2}^{\infty} \left\lfloor \frac{x}{p^k} \right\rfloor.$$

This probably needs some explanation. Although the double sum

$$\sum_{p \leq x} \sum_{k=1}^{\infty} \Lambda(p^k) \left\lfloor \frac{x}{p^k} \right\rfloor$$

Chapter 14: Estimating some sums

is actually taken over all possible prime powers p^k for any p not exceeding x, any terms for which $p^k > x$ contribute zero to the sum by virtue of the fact that

$$\left\lfloor \frac{x}{p^k} \right\rfloor = 0$$

in such cases. On the second line the double sum has been split up into two separate sums, one containing all the terms corresponding to primes not exceeding x, and the other containing the rest of the terms. From what you know about the 'big oh' notation, it should be reasonably clear that result (14.4) will have been shown to be true if it could be shown that

$$\sum_{p \leq x} \log p \sum_{k=2}^{\infty} \left\lfloor \frac{x}{p^k} \right\rfloor = O(x). \tag{14.7}$$

To this end, simple manipulations and the formula for the sum to infinity of a geometric progression lead to

$$\sum_{p \leq x} \log p \sum_{k=2}^{\infty} \left\lfloor \frac{x}{p^k} \right\rfloor \leq \sum_{p \leq x} \log p \sum_{k=2}^{\infty} \frac{x}{p^k}$$

$$= x \sum_{p \leq x} \log p \left(\frac{1}{p^2} \right) \left(1 + \frac{1}{p} + \frac{1}{p^2} + \ldots \right)$$

$$= x \sum_{p \leq x} \log p \left(\frac{1}{p^2} \right) \left(\frac{1}{1 - \frac{1}{p}} \right)$$

$$= x \sum_{p \leq x} \frac{\log p}{p(p-1)}.$$

Then, since

$$\sum_{p \leq x} \frac{\log p}{p(p-1)} < \sum_{n=2}^{\infty} \frac{\log n}{n(n-1)},$$

result (14.7) will have been shown to be true if it could be proved that the series

$$\sum_{n=2}^{\infty} \frac{\log n}{n(n-1)}$$

converges.

Now, on noting that $\frac{1}{n-1} \leq \frac{2}{n}$ for $n \geq 2$ and utilising a trick similar to the one that helped us to prove result (14.2) using rectangles, we have

$$\sum_{n=2}^{\infty} \frac{\log n}{n(n-1)} \leq \sum_{n=2}^{\infty} \frac{2 \log n}{n^2}$$

$$< \frac{\log 2}{2} + 2 \int_{2}^{\infty} \frac{\log t}{t^2} \, dt$$

$$= \frac{\log 2}{2} + 2 \left[-\frac{\log t}{t} - \frac{1}{t} \right]_{2}^{\infty}$$

$$= \frac{3 \log 2}{2} + 1$$

since $\frac{\log t}{t} \to 0$ as $t \to \infty$. This shows that

$$\sum_{n=2}^{\infty} \frac{\log n}{n(n-1)}$$

does indeed converge, and thus that result (14.7) holds. As noted previously, this implies the truth of result (14.4).

There is just one thing left to do in this chapter. We would like to show that result (14.4) is true even when we get rid of the floor function. This would give, after dividing both sides by x,

$$\sum_{p \leq x} \frac{\log p}{p} = \log x + O(1).$$

The result from the following challenge helps us to achieve this.

Challenge 14.2   Prove that

$$\left\lfloor \frac{x}{p} \right\rfloor - 2 \left\lfloor \frac{x}{2p} \right\rfloor$$

can only ever be 0 or 1.

Now, since

$$\left\lfloor \frac{x}{p} \right\rfloor - 2 \left\lfloor \frac{x}{2p} \right\rfloor$$

Chapter 14: Estimating some sums

only ever takes the values 0 or 1, and hence the sum

$$\sum_{p \leq \frac{x}{2}} \left(\left\lfloor \frac{x}{p} \right\rfloor - 2 \left\lfloor \frac{x}{2p} \right\rfloor \right) \log p$$

is non-negative, it follows that

$$\sum_{p \leq x} \left\lfloor \frac{x}{p} \right\rfloor \log p - 2 \sum_{p \leq \frac{x}{2}} \left\lfloor \frac{x}{2p} \right\rfloor \log p$$

$$= \sum_{p \leq \frac{x}{2}} \left(\left\lfloor \frac{x}{p} \right\rfloor - 2 \left\lfloor \frac{x}{2p} \right\rfloor \right) \log p + \sum_{\frac{x}{2} < p \leq x} \left\lfloor \frac{x}{p} \right\rfloor \log p$$

$$\geq \sum_{\frac{x}{2} < p \leq x} \left\lfloor \frac{x}{p} \right\rfloor \log p. \tag{14.8}$$

However,

$$\sum_{\frac{x}{2} < p \leq x} \left\lfloor \frac{x}{p} \right\rfloor \log p = \sum_{\frac{x}{2} < p \leq x} \log p$$

$$= \sum_{p \leq x} \log p - \sum_{p \leq \frac{x}{2}} \log p,$$

where the first step is as a consequence of the fact that

$$\left\lfloor \frac{x}{n} \right\rfloor = 1 \quad \text{when} \quad \frac{x}{2} < n \leq x.$$

This result, in conjunction with result (14.8), gives

$$\sum_{p \leq x} \left\lfloor \frac{x}{p} \right\rfloor \log p - 2 \sum_{p \leq \frac{x}{2}} \left\lfloor \frac{x}{2p} \right\rfloor \log p \geq \sum_{p \leq x} \log p - \sum_{p \leq \frac{x}{2}} \log p. \tag{14.9}$$

Next, using result (14.4), we have

$$\sum_{p \leq x} \left\lfloor \frac{x}{p} \right\rfloor \log p - 2 \sum_{p \leq \frac{x}{2}} \left\lfloor \frac{x}{2p} \right\rfloor \log p = x \log x + O(x) - 2 \left(\frac{x}{2} \log \frac{x}{2} + O\left(\frac{x}{2}\right) \right)$$

$$= x \log x - x \log \frac{x}{2} + O(x)$$

$$= x \log x - x \log x + x \log 2 + O(x)$$

$$= O(x).$$

On combining this result with result (14.9), it may be seen that there exists some positive real number M such that

$$\sum_{p \leq x} \log p - \sum_{p \leq \frac{x}{2}} \log p \leq Mx$$

for all $x \geq 2$. In fact, you will see that it is also true that

$$\sum_{p \leq \frac{x}{2}} \log p - \sum_{p \leq \frac{x}{4}} \log p \leq M\left(\frac{x}{2}\right),$$

$$\sum_{p \leq \frac{x}{4}} \log p - \sum_{p \leq \frac{x}{8}} \log p \leq M\left(\frac{x}{4}\right),$$

and so on, so that

$$\left(\sum_{p \leq x} \log p - \sum_{p \leq \frac{x}{2}} \log p\right) + \left(\sum_{p \leq \frac{x}{2}} \log p - \sum_{p \leq \frac{x}{4}} \log p\right)$$
$$+ \left(\sum_{p \leq \frac{x}{4}} \log p - \sum_{p \leq \frac{x}{8}} \log p\right) + \ldots \leq Mx\left(1 + \frac{1}{2} + \frac{1}{4} + \ldots\right),$$

which may be 'telescoped' to

$$\sum_{p \leq x} \log p \leq 2Mx \qquad (14.10)$$

on using the formula for the sum to infinity of a geometric progression and noting that

$$\sum_{p \leq \frac{x}{2^n}} \log p = 0 \quad \text{when} \quad \frac{x}{2^n} < 2.$$

It is obvious, from the definition of the floor function, that

$$\left\lfloor \frac{x}{n} \right\rfloor = \frac{x}{n} + O(1).$$

Therefore, on using result (14.10), it follows that

$$\sum_{p \leq x} \left\lfloor \frac{x}{p} \right\rfloor \log p = \sum_{p \leq x} \left(\frac{x}{p} + O(1) \right) \log p$$

$$= x \sum_{p \leq x} \frac{\log p}{p} + O\left(\sum_{p \leq x} \log p \right)$$

$$= x \sum_{p \leq x} \frac{\log p}{p} + O(x),$$

Combining this with result (14.4) and dividing both sides by x gives result (14.1), the result we have been striving for:

$$\sum_{p \leq x} \frac{\log p}{p} = \log x + O(1).$$

Exercise 14

1. In one of the steps in this chapter the following result was used without proof:

$$\sum_{n=2}^{\infty} \frac{2 \log n}{n^2} < \frac{\log 2}{2} + 2 \int_{2}^{\infty} \frac{\log t}{t^2} dt.$$

   Show that it is in fact true.

2. Use the 'rectangles trick' to obtain asymptotic formulae for:

   (a) $\sum_{n \leq x} \frac{1}{\sqrt{n}}$

   (b) $\sum_{n \leq x} n \log n.$

3. Result (14.1) tells us in some sense that we can use $\log x$ to approximate the sum

$$\sum_{p \leq x} \frac{\log p}{p}.$$

   What information does result (14.1) give us about the relative error in using this approximation as $x \to \infty$? How about the absolute error? You might like to use a piece of mathematical software such as *Mathematica*® to provide some numerical confirmation of your answers.

4. A result used earlier in this chapter is $\dfrac{\log t}{t} \to 0$ as $t \to \infty$. Is it in fact true that
$$\frac{(\log t)^n}{t} \to 0 \quad \text{as} \quad t \to \infty$$
for any given $n \in \mathbb{N}$? Justify your answer.

Chapter 15

The extraction process

Let us take stock of the current situation. In chapter 14 the following relation was established as result (14.1):

$$\sum_{p \leq x} \frac{\log p}{p} = \log x + O(1).$$

We noted at the time that although this might be of some interest in its own right, it is, as it stands, of no use to us whatsoever since the sum is evaluated over *all* primes no greater than x. Remember that we are only interested in the contribution made to the left-hand side of result (14.1) by those primes occurring in the arithmetic progression defined by $an + b$, $n = 0, 1, 2, \ldots$, where $\gcd(a, b) = 1$.

However, I did promise that there existed some mathematical trickery that would allow us to extract these terms from the left-hand side of result (14.1) in such a way as to leave something on the right-hand side that was still amenable to analysis. It might be a little too much to expect, however, that we will be left with an expression that is anything like as simple as $\log x + O(1)$! It is the Dirichlet characters and their orthogonality relations that, in keeping with our dentistry analogy in chapter 13, turn out to be the perfect tools for performing this extraction. Let us put $i = p$, $j = b$ and $k = a$ in result (9.3) on page 71 to give

$$\sum_{m=1}^{\phi(a)} \chi_m(p)\overline{\chi}_m(b) = \begin{cases} \phi(a) & \text{if } p \equiv b \pmod{a} \\ 0 & \text{otherwise,} \end{cases}$$

noting that:
(a) if $p = an + b$ then $p - b = an$ and thus $p \equiv b \pmod{a}$;
(b) the requirement for result (9.3) that $\gcd(p, a) = 1$ is automatically satisfied since $\gcd(a, b) = 1$ and $p \equiv b \pmod{a}$.

Next, multiply by $\frac{\log p}{p}$ and then sum over all primes $p \leq x$ to obtain

$$\sum_{p \leq x} \sum_{m=1}^{\phi(a)} \chi_m(p) \overline{\chi}_m(b) \frac{\log p}{p} = \phi(a) \sum_{\substack{p \leq x \\ p \equiv b \pmod{a}}} \frac{\log p}{p}. \qquad (15.1)$$

Since $\gcd(a, b) = 1$, the principal character χ_1 is such that $\chi_1(b) = 1$. It is also true that $\chi_1(p) = 0$ unless $\gcd(a, p) = 1$, in which case $\chi_1(p) = 1$. However, $\gcd(a, p) \neq 1$ if, and only if, $p \mid a$ so the double sum on the left-hand side of result (15.1) can be split up into two separate sums, one containing all the terms involving the principal character and the other containing the remaining terms, as follows:

$$\phi(a) \sum_{\substack{p \leq x \\ p \equiv b \pmod{a}}} \frac{\log p}{p} = \overline{\chi}_1(b) \sum_{p \leq x} \frac{\chi_1(p) \log p}{p} + \sum_{m=2}^{\phi(a)} \overline{\chi}_m(b) \sum_{p \leq x} \frac{\chi_m(p) \log p}{p}$$

$$= \sum_{\substack{p \leq x \\ \gcd(p,a)=1}} \frac{\log p}{p} + \sum_{m=2}^{\phi(a)} \overline{\chi}_m(b) \sum_{p \leq x} \frac{\chi_m(p) \log p}{p}$$

$$= \sum_{p \leq x} \frac{\log p}{p} - \sum_{\substack{p \leq x \\ p \mid a}} \frac{\log p}{p} + \sum_{m=2}^{\phi(a)} \overline{\chi}_m(b) \sum_{p \leq x} \frac{\chi_m(p) \log p}{p}$$

$$= \sum_{p \leq x} \frac{\log p}{p} + \sum_{m=2}^{\phi(a)} \overline{\chi}_m(b) \sum_{p \leq x} \frac{\chi_m(p) \log p}{p} + O(1), \qquad (15.2)$$

on noting that there are only finitely many primes p that divide a so that, for any x,

$$\sum_{\substack{p \leq x \\ p \mid a}} \frac{\log p}{p} \leq c$$

for some positive constant c.

Chapter 15: The extraction process 121

Since $O(1)$ divided by any non-zero constant is still $O(1)$, we obtain, on using result (15.2) in conjunction with result (14.1),

$$\sum_{\substack{p \leq x \\ p \equiv b \,(\text{mod } a)}} \frac{\log p}{p} = \frac{1}{\phi(a)} \log x + \frac{1}{\phi(a)} \sum_{m=2}^{\phi(a)} \overline{\chi}_m(b) \sum_{p \leq x} \frac{\chi_m(p) \log p}{p} + O(1).$$

(15.3)

At this point let us just step back and consider the above relation very carefully. We would like to be able to show that

$$\sum_{\substack{p \leq x \\ p \equiv b \,(\text{mod } a)}} \frac{\log p}{p} \to \infty \quad \text{as} \quad x \to \infty$$

since this would imply that there are infinitely primes p such that $p \equiv b$ (mod a), and hence that there are infinitely many primes in the arithmetic progression $an + b$, $n = 0, 1, 2, \ldots$. In order to achieve this, since $\log x \to \infty$ as $x \to \infty$, it would be enough to show that

$$\sum_{m=2}^{\phi(a)} \overline{\chi}_m(b) \sum_{p \leq x} \frac{\chi_m(p) \log p}{p} = O(1)$$

since this would imply, via result (15.3), that

$$\sum_{\substack{p \leq x \\ p \equiv b \,(\text{mod } a)}} \frac{\log p}{p} = \frac{1}{\phi(a)} \log x + O(1).$$

However,

$$\sum_{m=2}^{\phi(a)} \overline{\chi}_m(b) \sum_{p \leq x} \frac{\chi_m(p) \log p}{p}$$

is just a finite sum of terms of the form

$$\overline{\chi}_m(b) \sum_{p \leq x} \frac{\chi_m(p) \log p}{p}$$

where χ_m is a non-principal character. It would therefore be possible to complete the proof of Dirichlet's theorem if it could be shown that

$$\sum_{p \leq x} \frac{\chi_m(p) \log p}{p} = O(1) \tag{15.4}$$

for each $m = 2, 3, \ldots, \phi(a)$.

Our goal from now on is thus to show that result (15.4) is in fact true. As you will see, this is not an entirely straightforward matter. Indeed, there are still many mathematical twists and turns to negotiate.

Chapter 16

Rearranging a sum

You may have noticed that the form of the Dirichlet L-function

$$L'_m = -\sum_{n=1}^{\infty} \frac{\chi_m(n)\log n}{n},$$

as given in Chapter 10, is remarkably similar to that of the sums on the left-hand side of (15.4):

$$\sum_{p\leq x} \frac{\chi_m(p)\log p}{p}.$$

It is apparent, however, that L'_m
 (a) is summed to infinity rather than just up to x;
 (b) is summed over all positive integers rather just over the primes;
 (c) has a negative sign.

The function L'_m effectively provides a bridge connecting the sums

$$\sum_{p\leq x} \frac{\chi_m(p)\log p}{p},$$

whose terms are summed over all primes no greater than x, to certain new sums, whose terms are summed over all integers no greater than x, given by

$$\sum_{n\leq x} \frac{\mu(n)\chi_m(n)}{n},$$

where μ is the Möbius function, introduced in Chapter 11.

To establish this connection will be the focus of the current chapter. The relationship between the two sums will be obtained by rearranging the sum

$$\sum_{n\leq x} \frac{\chi_m(n)\Lambda(n)}{n} \qquad (16.1)$$

in two different ways and then equating the resultant expressions. Remember that Λ is Mangoldt's function, defined in Chapter 11.

First, from the definition of Λ, it follows that

$$\sum_{n\leq x} \frac{\chi_m(n)\Lambda(n)}{n} = \sum_{p\leq x} \sum_{k=1}^{c(x,p)} \frac{\chi_m(p^k)\log p}{p^k}$$

$$= \sum_{p\leq x} \frac{\chi_m(p)\log p}{p} + \sum_{p\leq x} \sum_{k=2}^{c(x,p)} \frac{\chi_m(p^k)\log p}{p^k},$$

where

$$c = c(x,p) = \left\lfloor \frac{\log x}{\log p} \right\rfloor$$

gives the exponent of the highest power of p less than or equal to x; in other words, $p^c \leq x < p^{c+1}$.

Challenge 16.1 Although it all looks innocent enough, there is rather a lot going on in the above rearrangement of (16.1). Therefore, before going any further, spend some time convincing yourself of the validity of each step.

Now consider the final double sum above. On making use of the triangle inequality (see Challenge 7.2), we obtain

$$\left| \sum_{p\leq x} \sum_{k=2}^{c} \frac{\chi_m(p^k)\log p}{p^k} \right| \leq \sum_{p\leq x} \log p \sum_{k=2}^{c} \frac{|\chi_m(p^k)|}{p^k}$$

$$\leq \sum_{p\leq x} \log p \sum_{k=2}^{c} \frac{1}{p^k}$$

$$< \sum_{p\leq x} \log p \sum_{k=2}^{\infty} \frac{1}{p^k},$$

Chapter 16: Rearranging a sum

remembering that $|\chi_m(n)| = 1$ or $\chi_m(n) = 0$. However, by referring back to the working used to establish (14.7), it can be seen that

$$\sum_{p \leq x} \log p \sum_{k=2}^{\infty} \frac{1}{p^k} = O(1),$$

leading to the result

$$\sum_{p \leq x} \frac{\chi_m(p) \log p}{p} = \sum_{n \leq x} \frac{\chi_m(n) \Lambda(n)}{n} + O(1). \tag{16.2}$$

Let us next express

$$\sum_{n \leq x} \frac{\chi_m(n) \Lambda(n)}{n}$$

in a different way. First, by way of (11.4), a result obtained using the Möbius inversion formula, it follows that

$$\sum_{n \leq x} \frac{\chi_m(n) \Lambda(n)}{n} = \sum_{n \leq x} \frac{\chi_m(n)}{n} \sum_{d|n} \mu(d) \log\left(\frac{n}{d}\right).$$

Then, since χ_m is multiplicative, we obtain

$$\sum_{n \leq x} \frac{\chi_m(n)}{n} \sum_{d|n} \mu(d) \log\left(\frac{n}{d}\right) = \sum_{kd \leq x} \frac{\chi_m(kd)}{kd} \mu(d) \log\left(\frac{kd}{d}\right)$$

$$= \sum_{kd \leq x} \frac{\mu(d) \chi_m(d) \chi_m(k) \log k}{kd}$$

$$= \sum_{d \leq x} \frac{\mu(d) \chi_m(d)}{d} \sum_{k \leq \frac{x}{d}} \frac{\chi_m(k) \log k}{k}. \tag{16.3}$$

Challenge 16.2 Once more we encounter some manipulations that are not totally straightforward. Go through the derivation of (16.3) line by line to ensure you understand every detail.

Thus far, χ_m could have been any Dirichlet character. Now we assume it to be non-principal, in which case (10.4), in conjunction with (16.3), gives

$$\sum_{n \leq x} \frac{\chi_m(n) \Lambda(n)}{n} = \sum_{d \leq x} \frac{\mu(d) \chi_m(d)}{d} \left\{ -L'_m + O\left(\frac{\log(\frac{x}{d})}{(\frac{x}{d})} \right) \right\}$$

$$= -L'_m \sum_{d \leq x} \frac{\mu(d) \chi_m(d)}{d} + O\left(\sum_{d \leq x} \frac{\log(\frac{x}{d})}{x} \right),$$

where, in the last step, the obvious fact that $|\mu(d) \chi_m(d)| \leq 1$ has been used in order to obtain the function under the 'big oh'.

However

$$\sum_{d \leq x} \frac{\log(\frac{x}{d})}{x} = \frac{1}{x} \left(\sum_{d \leq x} \log x - \sum_{d \leq x} \log d \right)$$

$$= \frac{1}{x} \left(\lfloor x \rfloor \log x - (x \log x - x + O(\log x)) \right)$$

$$= \frac{1}{x} (x + (\lfloor x \rfloor - x) \log x + O(\log x))$$

$$= \frac{1}{x} (x + O(1) \log x + O(\log x))$$

$$= O(1), \tag{16.4}$$

remembering that it has already shown that

$$\sum_{n \leq x} \log n = x \log x - x + O(\log x)$$

when obtaining (14.3) via the 'rectangles trick'.

Challenge 16.3 I have left out a couple of steps of working (on purpose) to get to $O(1)$ in Result 16.4. It will be a good test of your knowledge of the floor function and the 'big oh' notation to fill in the precise details.

It has thus been established that

$$\sum_{n \leq x} \frac{\chi_m(n) \Lambda(n)}{n} = -L'_m \sum_{d \leq x} \frac{\mu(d) \chi_m(d)}{d} + O(1).$$

Chapter 16: Rearranging a sum

Then, on using this with (16.2), we obtain

$$\sum_{p \leq x} \frac{\chi_m(p) \log p}{p} = -L'_m \sum_{n \leq x} \frac{\mu(n)\chi_m(n)}{n} + O(1) \qquad (16.5)$$

noting, of course, that it does not matter which letter is use as the indexing variable in the sum on the right-hand side; it could be n or d or any other variable that was not being used to represent something else in the relation!

If it could be shown that

$$\sum_{n \leq x} \frac{\mu(n)\chi_m(n)}{n} = O(1)$$

for each non-principal character χ_m then (16.5) would be enough to imply that

$$\sum_{p \leq x} \frac{\chi_m(p) \log p}{p} = O(1), \quad m = 2, 3, \ldots, \phi(a),$$

which is exactly what we are trying to prove! It is in fact possible to obtain the asymptotic relations

$$\sum_{n \leq x} \frac{\mu(n)\chi_m(n)}{n} = O(1), \quad m = 2, 3, \ldots, \phi(a)$$

via the generalised Möbius inversion formula. We go part of the way towards achieving this in the next chapter.

Chapter 17

Showing that L_m is not zero

We now know that all we have to do is to demonstrate the truth of the asymptotic relations

$$\sum_{n \leq x} \frac{\mu(n)\chi_m(n)}{n} = O(1), \quad m = 2, 3, \ldots, \phi(a).$$

In order to make some progress in this direction we will use the generalised Möbius inversion formula to help obtain the following result, noting carefully that it involves L_m rather than the L'_m of result (16.5) on page 127:

$$L_m \sum_{n \leq x} \frac{\mu(n)\chi_m(n)}{n} = O(1). \quad (17.1)$$

Supposing result (17.1) to be true, then

$$\sum_{n \leq x} \frac{\mu(n)\chi_m(n)}{n} = O(1), \quad m = 2, 3, \ldots, \phi(a),$$

so long as L_m is not zero, $m = 2, 3, \ldots, \phi(a)$. There lies another problem! How can we be sure that $L_m \neq 0$ for each non-principal character? I do not blame you if, by now, you are starting to feel a certain amount of frustration at the fact that each new idea we come up with seems to create yet more problems; it might appear that this could continue indefinitely. Let me assure you then that this latest difficulty can be overcome, albeit with a fair amount of effort, so let us put it aside for the moment, and concentrate first on trying to obtain result (17.1).

From definitions 8.1 and 9.4 on page 60 and on page 70 it is clear that Dirichlet characters are, when treated as arithmetic functions, completely multiplicative. It is therefore possible to use them in the generalised Möbius inversion formula. On putting $\alpha(n) = \chi_m(n)$ and $F(x) = x$ into result (12.3) on page 98, we obtain

$$x = \sum_{n \leq x} \mu(n) \chi_m(n) G\left(\frac{x}{n}\right),$$

where

$$G(x) = \sum_{n \leq x} \chi_m(n) \left(\frac{x}{n}\right)$$
$$= x \sum_{n \leq x} \frac{\chi_m(n)}{n}.$$

However, it has already been shown, via result (10.2) on page 81, that $G(x) = xL_m + O(1)$. Therefore

$$x = \sum_{n \leq x} \mu(n) \chi_m(n) \left(\frac{xL_m}{n} + O(1)\right)$$
$$= xL_m \sum_{n \leq x} \frac{\mu(n)\chi_m(n)}{n} + O(x),$$

where, in the final step, we have used the result

$$\sum_{n \leq x} \mu(n) \chi_m(n) = O(x),$$

which is itself a consequence of the obvious fact that $|\mu(n)\chi_m(n)| \leq 1$ for all positive integers n. From this it follows that

$$L_m \sum_{n \leq x} \frac{\mu(n)\chi_m(n)}{n} = O(1),$$

as required.

We are now left with the task of showing that $L_m \neq 0$ for all non-principal characters χ_m. In the remainder of this chapter we go part of the way to proving this by showing that it is in fact true for all *real-valued characters*, where a character χ_m is known as real-valued if $\chi_m(n) \in \mathbb{R}$ for all $n \in \mathbb{N}$. It will be found expedient to define some new functions

Chapter 17: Showing that L_m is not zero

along the way. The purpose of these functions might be far from obvious initially, but all will become clear.

First, let
$$A(n) = \sum_{d|n} \chi(d)$$
where χ is a real-valued character modulo k. If n is a prime power, say $n = p^m$, then
$$A(n) = A(p^m)$$
$$= \sum_{j=0}^{m} \chi(p^j)$$
$$= 1 + \sum_{j=1}^{m} \{\chi(p)\}^j,$$

where the last step is as a consequence of the fact that characters are multiplicative. Since χ is real-valued, $\chi(p)$, as either a root of unity or zero, can only be equal to either 1, 0 or -1. From the above result it can be seen that if $\chi(p) = 0$ then $A(p^m) = 1$, if $\chi(p) = 1$ then $A(p^m) = 1 + m$ while if $\chi(p) = -1$ then $A(p^m) = 1$ if m is even and $A(p^m) = 0$ if m is odd. From this it follows that $A(p^m) \geq 0$ in general and $A(p^m) \geq 1$ if m is even.

The fact that χ is multiplicative implies that A is also multiplicative, as is now shown. With $\gcd(m, n) = 1$ then
$$A(mn) = \sum_{d|mn} \chi(d)$$
$$= \sum_{\substack{d_1|m \\ d_2|n}} \chi(d_1 d_2)$$
$$= \sum_{\substack{d_1|m \\ d_2|n}} \chi(d_1)\chi(d_2)$$
$$= \left(\sum_{d_1|m} \chi(d_1)\right)\left(\sum_{d_2|n} \chi(d_2)\right)$$
$$= A(m)A(n).$$

In the second and third lines above, the sum is taken over all possible pairs (d_1, d_2) such that $d_1|m$ and $d_2|n$. The assumption that $\gcd(m, n) = 1$

implies $\gcd(d_1, d_2) = 1$ in the second line, thereby allowing us to write $\chi(d_1 d_2) = \chi(d_1)\chi(d_2)$ in proceeding from the second to the third line.

Now say that n has the prime factorisation given by

$$n = p_1^{a_1} p_2^{a_2} \cdots p_r^{a_r}.$$

The multiplicative property of A is used to obtain

$$A(n) = A(p_1^{a_1}) A(p_2^{a_2}) \cdots A(p_r^{a_r}).$$

Since we have already shown that each of the factors on the right-hand side is non-negative, we know that $A(n) \geq 0$ for all positive integers n. Also, if n is a square then each a_i is even. As $A(p^m) \geq 1$ if m is even, it is the case that each of these factors is at least 1, so that $A(n) \geq 1$ if n is a square.

Now let

$$B(x) = \sum_{n \leq x} \frac{A(n)}{\sqrt{n}}.$$

It is easy to show that $B(x) \to \infty$ as $x \to \infty$. For, from the results above concerning $A(n)$, it follows that

$$\sum_{n \leq x} \frac{A(n)}{\sqrt{n}} \geq \sum_{\substack{n \leq x \\ n = m^2}} \frac{1}{\sqrt{n}}$$

$$= \sum_{m \leq \sqrt{x}} \frac{1}{m}.$$

Then, remembering that in Chapter 3 we established the divergence of the harmonic series,

$$\sum_{n=1}^{\infty} \frac{1}{n} = 1 + \frac{1}{2} + \frac{1}{3} + \frac{1}{4} + \cdots,$$

it must therefore be the case that $B(x) \to \infty$ as $x \to \infty$.

Next we show that $B(x) = 2L\sqrt{x} + O(1)$ for all $x \geq 1$ (remember that for the Dirichlet L-function of a character without a subscript we may, without ambiguity, write L for $\sum_{n=1}^{\infty} \frac{\chi(n)}{n}$). Since $B(x) \to \infty$ as $x \to \infty$, if it is true that $B(x) = 2L\sqrt{x} + O(1)$, then it must be the case that $2L\sqrt{x} + O(1) \to \infty$ as $x \to \infty$. However, $O(1)$ is bounded, so that it must also be true that $2L\sqrt{x} \to \infty$, which in turn implies that $L \neq 0$.

Chapter 17: Showing that L_m is not zero

This result implies that $L_m \neq 0$ when χ_m is a real-valued non-principal Dirichlet character.

We can rewrite $B(x)$ as follows:

$$B(x) = \sum_{n \leq x} \frac{A(n)}{\sqrt{n}}$$

$$= \sum_{n \leq x} \frac{1}{\sqrt{n}} \sum_{d|n} \chi(d)$$

$$= \sum_{n \leq x} \sum_{d|n} \frac{\chi(d)}{\sqrt{n}}$$

$$= \sum_{qd \leq x} \frac{\chi(d)}{\sqrt{qd}}$$

$$= \sum_{qd \leq x} \left(\frac{1}{\sqrt{q}}\right)\left(\frac{\chi(d)}{\sqrt{d}}\right), \qquad (17.2)$$

where in the last two sums the summation is over all q and d such that $qd \leq x$. If you are not entirely sure how to get from the third to the fourth line above, then have another look at challenge 16.2 on page 125.

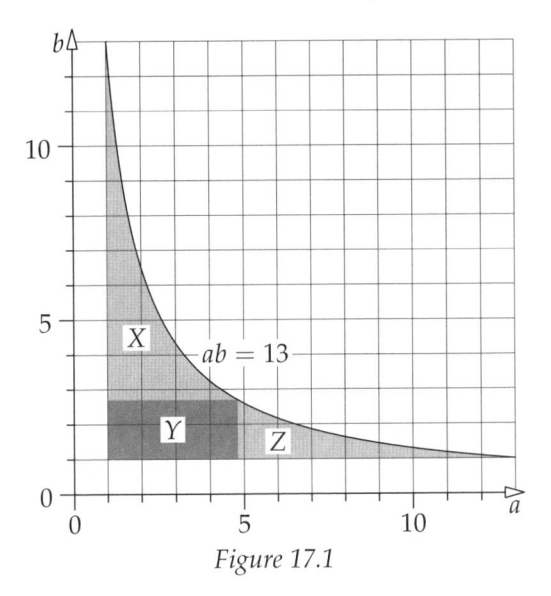

Figure 17.1

In order to arrange the sum (17.2) into something more useful to us, it is worth considering figure 17.1. This shows the curve defined by $ab = 13$ and also sections of the lines

$$a = 1, \quad a = \frac{130}{27}, \quad b = 1 \text{ and } b = \frac{27}{10}.$$

(There is nothing special about the choice of $a = \frac{130}{27}$ and $b = \frac{27}{10}$ other than the fact that $\frac{130}{27} \times \frac{27}{10} = 13$.) It may be seen that $B(13)$ is actually the expression

$$\left(\frac{1}{\sqrt{a}}\right)\left(\frac{\chi(b)}{\sqrt{b}}\right)$$

summed at all lattice points (integer coordinates) contained in, and on the boundary of, the region enclosed by the curve $ab = 13$ and the lines $a = 1$ and $b = 1$. One way of obtaining this sum is to evaluate at all lattice points contained in the region defined by the union of X and Y, then evaluate it all lattice points contained in the region defined by the union of Y and Z, add these together and then subtract the sum evaluated at all lattice points in Y (as these will have been double-counted). This gives

$$B(13) = \sum_{n \leq \frac{130}{27}} \frac{1}{\sqrt{n}} \sum_{m \leq \frac{13}{n}} \frac{\chi(m)}{\sqrt{m}} + \sum_{n \leq \frac{27}{10}} \frac{\chi(n)}{\sqrt{n}} \sum_{m \leq \frac{13}{n}} \frac{1}{\sqrt{m}}$$

$$- \left(\sum_{n \leq \frac{130}{27}} \frac{1}{\sqrt{n}}\right) \left(\sum_{n \leq \frac{27}{10}} \frac{\chi(n)}{\sqrt{n}}\right),$$

which generalises to

$$B(x) = \sum_{n \leq a} \frac{1}{\sqrt{n}} \sum_{m \leq \frac{x}{n}} \frac{\chi(m)}{\sqrt{m}} + \sum_{n \leq b} \frac{\chi(n)}{\sqrt{n}} \sum_{m \leq \frac{x}{n}} \frac{1}{\sqrt{m}}$$

$$- \left(\sum_{n \leq a} \frac{1}{\sqrt{n}}\right) \left(\sum_{n \leq b} \frac{\chi(n)}{\sqrt{n}}\right), \quad (17.3)$$

where $a > 1, b > 1$ and $ab = x$.

From question 2(a) of exercise 14 (see page 117) it follows that

$$\sum_{n \leq x} \frac{1}{\sqrt{n}} = 2\sqrt{x} + O(1). \quad (17.4)$$

Also, the fact that
$$\sum_{n=1}^{\infty} \frac{\chi_m(n)}{\sqrt{n}}$$
converges for all non-principal characters and that
$$\sum_{n \leq x} \frac{\chi_m(n)}{\sqrt{n}} = \sum_{n=1}^{\infty} \frac{\chi_m(n)}{\sqrt{n}} + O\left(\frac{1}{\sqrt{x}}\right)$$
(see results (10.3) and (10.5) on page 81) means that we may write
$$\sum_{n \leq x} \frac{\chi_m(n)}{\sqrt{n}} = C + O\left(\frac{1}{\sqrt{x}}\right) \tag{17.5}$$
for some constant C.

Now, on putting $a = b = \sqrt{x}$ in result (17.3), and then using results (17.4) and (17.5), it is possible, with a bit of care and patience, to obtain the relation $B(x) = 2L\sqrt{x} + O(1)$ promised earlier. What follows might seem a little daunting at first, but please stick with it, and go through each and every step. Before you start you might need to remind yourself about 'big oh' and its properties, as considerable use is made of this when simplifying the expression for $B(x)$.

$$B(x) = \sum_{n \leq \sqrt{x}} \frac{1}{\sqrt{n}} \sum_{m \leq \frac{x}{n}} \frac{\chi(m)}{\sqrt{m}} + \sum_{n \leq \sqrt{x}} \frac{\chi(n)}{\sqrt{n}} \sum_{m \leq \frac{x}{n}} \frac{1}{\sqrt{m}}$$
$$- \left(\sum_{n \leq \sqrt{x}} \frac{1}{\sqrt{n}}\right)\left(\sum_{n \leq \sqrt{x}} \frac{\chi(n)}{\sqrt{n}}\right)$$
$$= \sum_{n \leq \sqrt{x}} \frac{1}{\sqrt{n}}\left(C + \sqrt{\frac{n}{x}}\right) + \sum_{n \leq \sqrt{x}} \frac{\chi(n)}{\sqrt{n}}\left(2\sqrt{\frac{x}{n}} + O(1)\right)$$
$$- \left(2x^{\frac{1}{4}} + O(1)\right)\left(C + O\left(\frac{1}{x^{\frac{1}{4}}}\right)\right)$$
$$= C \sum_{n \leq \sqrt{x}} \frac{1}{\sqrt{n}} + \frac{1}{\sqrt{x}} \sum_{n \leq \sqrt{x}} 1 + 2\sqrt{x} \sum_{n \leq \sqrt{x}} \frac{\chi(n)}{n} + O(1) \sum_{n \leq \sqrt{x}} \frac{\chi(n)}{\sqrt{n}}$$
$$- 2Cx^{\frac{1}{4}} - O(1)(C + 1) - O\left(\frac{1}{x^{\frac{1}{4}}}\right).$$

The above can be simplified, using results (17.4) and (17.5) once more and result (10.2) on page 81, to obtain

$$B(x) = C\left(2x^{\frac{1}{4}} + O(1)\right) + O(1) + 2\sqrt{x}\left(L + O\left(\frac{1}{\sqrt{x}}\right)\right)$$
$$+ O(1)\left(C + O\left(\frac{1}{x^{\frac{1}{4}}}\right)\right) - 2Cx^{\frac{1}{4}}$$
$$= 2L\sqrt{x} + O(1).$$

So we now know that $L_m \neq 0$ for all real-valued non-principal characters χ_m. In the next chapter it is shown that L_m is also non-zero whenever χ_m is a not a real-valued character, thereby proving Dirichlet's theorem. By a *complex-valued character* χ_m we mean that there exists some $n \in \mathbb{N}$ such that the imaginary part of $\chi_m(n)$ is non-zero. Note that the principal character is not complex-valued.

Chapter 18

The final step

When wading through a mass of symbols, it is sometimes easy to lose sight of exactly what it is we are trying to prove. In order really to revel in the last step of the proof, let us make absolutely sure that we have a clear overall picture of what we need to do and how we are going to do it. After a lot of hard work, we have got to the stage where, in order to prove Dirichlet's theorem on primes in arithmetic progressions, it just needs to be shown that $L_m \neq 0$ for all complex-valued characters χ_m (bearing in mind that this was shown to be true for all real-valued non-principal Dirichlet characters in chapter 17). This is because, from result (15.3) onwards, we have managed to establish the following chain of implications:

$L_m \neq 0$ for all non-principal Dirichlet characters χ_m

$$\Rightarrow \sum_{n \leq x} \frac{\mu(n)\chi_m(n)}{n} = O(1), \quad m = 2, 3, \ldots, \phi(a)$$

$$\Rightarrow \sum_{p \leq x} \frac{\chi_m(p) \log p}{p} = O(1), \quad m = 2, 3, \ldots, \phi(a)$$

$$\Rightarrow \sum_{\substack{p \leq x \\ p \equiv b \pmod{a}}} \frac{\log p}{p} = \frac{1}{\phi(a)} \log x + O(1)$$

$$\Rightarrow \sum_{\substack{p \leq x \\ p \equiv b \pmod{a}}} \frac{\log p}{p} \to \infty \quad \text{as} \quad x \to \infty.$$

The approach that is going to be taken in this final step of the proof is to assume that there does actually exist at least one complex-valued non-principal character χ_m such that $L_m = 0$, and then see what would result as a consequence. It turns out that, in making this assumption, we are eventually led to conclude that there exists some positive real number, t say, such that the sum

$$\sum_{\substack{p \leq x \\ p \equiv 1 \pmod{a}}} \frac{\log p}{p}$$

is negative for all $x > t$. This, however, is clearly nonsense! The initial assumption must therefore have been false, showing that $L_m \neq 0$ for all complex-valued characters χ_m, as required. In other words, we will be using proof by contradiction to deliver the *coup de grâce*.

First, a result is obtained that will play a part in establishing the contradiction being sought. Utilising result (12.3) on page 98, we obtain from the generalised Möbius inversion formula, with $\alpha(n) = \chi_m(n)$ and $F(x) = x \log x$,

$$x \log x = \sum_{n \leq x} \mu(n) \chi_m(n) G\left(\frac{x}{n}\right),$$

where

$$G(x) = \sum_{n \leq x} \chi_m(n) \left(\frac{x}{n}\right)(\log x - \log n)$$

$$= x \log x \sum_{n \leq x} \frac{\chi_m(n)}{n} - x \sum_{n \leq x} \frac{\chi_m(n) \log n}{n}$$

$$= x \log x \left(L_m + O\left(\frac{1}{x}\right)\right) + x \left(L'_m + O\left(\frac{\log x}{x}\right)\right),$$

on using results (10.2) and (10.4) on page 81 in the final step. If it is assumed that $L_m = 0$ then $G(x) = xL'_m + O(\log x)$. In this case

$$x \log x = \sum_{n \leq x} \mu(n) \chi_m(n) \left(\frac{xL'_m}{n} + O\left(\log\left(\frac{x}{n}\right)\right)\right)$$

$$= xL'_m \sum_{n \leq x} \frac{\mu(n) \chi_m(n)}{n} + O\left(\sum_{n \leq x} \mu(n) \chi_m(n) \log\left(\frac{x}{n}\right)\right)$$

$$= xL'_m \sum_{n \leq x} \frac{\mu(n) \chi_m(n)}{n} + O(x).$$

Chapter 18: The final step

This last step can be justified since $|\mu(n)\chi_m(n)| \leq 1$ for all positive integers n, and, as is implied by result (16.4) on page 126,

$$\sum_{n \leq x} \log\left(\frac{x}{n}\right) = O(x).$$

Thus the assumption that $L_m = 0$ leads to the result

$$L'_m \sum_{n \leq x} \frac{\mu(n)\chi_m(n)}{n} = \log x + O(1). \tag{18.1}$$

On the other hand, if it is now assumed that $L_m \neq 0$, it follows, on using result (17.1) on page 129, that

$$\sum_{n \leq x} \frac{\mu(n)\chi_m(n)}{n} = O(1).$$

Thus $L_m \neq 0$ implies that

$$L'_m \sum_{n \leq x} \frac{\mu(n)\chi_m(n)}{n} = O(1). \tag{18.2}$$

Next, with $b = 1$ in result (15.3) on page 121, remembering that $\overline{\chi}_m(1) = 1$, we obtain

$$\sum_{\substack{p \leq x \\ p \equiv 1 \pmod{a}}} \frac{\log p}{p} = \frac{1}{\phi(a)} \log x + \frac{1}{\phi(a)} \sum_{m=2}^{\phi(a)} \sum_{p \leq x} \frac{\chi_m(p) \log p}{p} + O(1). \tag{18.3}$$

Then, on using result (16.5) on page 127 in conjunction with result (18.3), it follows that

$$\sum_{\substack{p \leq x \\ p \equiv 1 \pmod{a}}} \frac{\log p}{p} = \frac{1}{\phi(a)} \log x + \frac{1}{\phi(a)} \sum_{m=2}^{\phi(a)} \left(-L'_m \sum_{n \leq x} \frac{\mu(n)\chi_m(n)}{n} + O(1) \right) + O(1).$$

This last expression can be written as

$$\frac{1}{\phi(a)} \log x - \frac{1}{\phi(a)} \left(\sum_i L'_i \sum_{n \leq x} \frac{\mu(n)\chi_i(n)}{n} + \sum_j L'_j \sum_{n \leq x} \frac{\mu(n)\chi_j(n)}{n} \right) + O(1),$$

where the first sum in the brackets is taken over all non-principal characters χ_i for which $L_i = 0$, and the second sum is taken over all non-principal characters χ_j for which $L_j \neq 0$. Using the above, along with results (18.1) and (18.2), gives rise to

$$\sum_{\substack{p \leq x \\ p \equiv 1 \,(\mathrm{mod}\, a)}} \frac{\log p}{p} = \frac{1}{\phi(a)} \log x - \frac{1}{\phi(a)} \left(\sum_i (\log x + O(1)) + \sum_j O(1) \right) + O(1)$$

$$= \frac{1}{\phi(a)} \log x - \frac{N(a) \log x}{\phi(a)} + O(1)$$

$$= \left(\frac{1 - N(a)}{\phi(a)} \right) \log x + O(1),$$

where $N(a)$ is the number of distinct non-principal characters χ_i modulo a such that $L_i = 0$.

We already know that $L_m \neq 0$ if χ_m is a real-valued non-principal character, so if L_m does equal zero then χ_m is complex-valued. Furthermore, it follows from the work carried out in chapter 9 that if χ_m is a character then $\overline{\chi}_m$ is also a character. If χ_m is complex-valued then $\overline{\chi}_m$ will be distinct from χ_m. It is also clear, from the definition

$$L_m = \sum_{n=1}^{\infty} \frac{\chi_m(n)}{n},$$

that $L_m = 0$ if, and only if, $\overline{L}_m = 0$, where $\overline{L}_m$ denotes

$$\sum_{n=1}^{\infty} \frac{\overline{\chi}_m(n)}{n}.$$

Thus the only characters χ_m for which $L_m = 0$ are complex-valued and occur in complex conjugate pairs, so that $N(a)$ is even. This means that if at least one such character exists then $N(a) \geq 2$. However, if $N(a) \geq 2$ then

$$\left(\frac{1 - N(a)}{\phi(a)} \right) \log x + O(1)$$

will be negative for sufficiently large x, whereas

$$\sum_{\substack{p \leq x \\ p \equiv 1 \,(\mathrm{mod}\, a)}} \frac{\log p}{p}$$

is certainly non-negative. This contradiction tells us that the assumption concerning the existence of at least one non-principal character χ_m for which $L_m = 0$ must be false, as required.

WE HAVE DONE IT!

Chapter 19

Afterword

Hopefully you will want to go ahead and do a bit of independent reading around this fascinating area of mathematics. Here are some further results, points of interest and applications of the theorem that are well worth looking up.

1. You might ask what the record is for the number of consecutive terms of an arithmetic progression that are all prime? Well, the sequence $5, 11, 17, 23, 29\ldots$ tells us that the record must be at least 5. In fact, it does not take too much effort to double that record. The following gives a 10-term arithmetic progression of primes with a common difference of 210:

   $199, 409, 619, 829, 1039, 1249, 1459, 1669, 1879, 2089.$

   At the time of writing the record is 26. It was discovered by Benoat Perichon in 2010, see [27].
   Until relatively recently, it was not known whether the primes contain arbitrarily long arithmetic progressions. This matter has now been settled. Ben Green and Terence Tao gave a proof, in 2004, that the prime numbers do actually contain arithmetic progressions of length k for all positive integers k [16]. However, their proof does not tell us how to find these arithmetic progressions!
   A special case of the situation in which the consecutive terms of an arithmetic progression are all prime occurs when these terms are themselves consecutive primes. In other words, we are no longer allowing primes to occur between the terms of the progression. At

the time of writing the largest known sequence of consecutive primes in arithmetic progression has 10 terms.

2. We proved Dirichlet's theorem on primes in arithmetic progressions by showing that

$$\sum_{\substack{p \leq x \\ p \equiv b \pmod{a}}} \frac{\log p}{p} = \frac{1}{\phi(a)} \log x + O(1).$$

However, you may have spotted that this asymptotic relation does actually imply more than just Dirichlet's theorem. Note that the right-hand side is independent of b and that every sufficiently large prime number is congruent modulo a to some b coprime to a. This tells us that the primes in each of the $\phi(a)$ reduced residue classes modulo a make roughly the same contribution to the sum

$$\sum_{p \leq x} \frac{\log p}{p}.$$

Unfortunately, we cannot immediately infer from this that the *number* of primes no greater than x in each of the reduced residue classes is roughly the same. This is because we cannot rule out, without further analysis, the possibility that the function $f(n) = \frac{\log n}{n}$ allows the primes no greater than x to be partitioned amongst the reduced residue classes in such a way that the numbers of primes in each of these classes is quite different but the contributions from the primes to the above sum is roughly the same for each class.

However, our relation would at least seem to make plausible the possibility that the primes are roughly equally distributed amongst the reduced residue classes. Indeed, this does actually turn out to be the case. A proof is given in [12] of the fact that if $\gcd(a,b) = 1$ then $\pi_b(x)$, the number of primes p less than x and satisfying $p \equiv b \pmod{a}$, is given by the asymptotic formula

$$\pi_b(x) \sim \frac{x}{\phi(a) \log x},$$

which is mathematical shorthand for

$$\lim_{x \to \infty} \frac{\pi_b(x)}{\left(\frac{x}{\phi(a) \log x}\right)} = 1.$$

The arithmetic progression $16, 25, 34, 43, \ldots$, for example, contains approximately one sixth of the primes since $\phi(9) = 6$.

3. A Russian mathematician named Yuri Vladimirovich Linnik (1915–1972) came up with an interesting result in connection with Dirichlet's theorem on primes in arithmetic progressions. He considered the problem of finding the smallest prime in the arithmetic progression defined by $an + b$, $n = 1, 2, 3, \ldots$. Denoting this prime by $p(a, b)$, Linnik showed in 1944 that there exist positive numbers c and L such that

$$p(a, b) < ca^L$$

for any choice of positive integers a and b satisfying $1 \leq b \leq a$ and $\gcd(a, b) = 1$.

We would of course like to have an idea of just how small we can make c and L. For the special case $a = b = 1$ we have $p(a, b) = 2$ and $ca^L = c$, in which case any $c > 2$ will suffice. However, if we assume that $a \geq 2$ then we may set $c = 1$ and look for the smallest L such that $p(a, b) < a^L$ is always satisfied. The least possible value of L is called Linnik's constant, and it is known that this is no greater than $5\frac{1}{5}$, see [26].

4. If you are feeling particularly ambitious and would like to take on an even more demanding project than Dirichlet's theorem, then you might consider tackling the *prime number theorem*. This famous theorem concerns the function $\pi(x)$, giving the number of primes less than or equal to the positive real number x, something we mentioned briefly in chapter 4. For example, $\pi\left(14\frac{2}{9}\right) = 6$ since there are 6 primes less than or equal to $14\frac{2}{9}$, namely 2, 3, 5, 7, 11 and 13. We already know that $\pi(x) \to \infty$ as $x \to \infty$, but the prime number theorem actually gives us information on how $\pi(x)$ tends to infinity. It provides us with the following asymptotic formula for $\pi(x)$:

$$\pi(x) \sim \frac{x}{\log x}.$$

This result was proved by Jacques Hadamard and Charles de la Vallée Poussin in 1896, although independently of one another. Their proofs were achieved by utilising the properties of the *Riemann zeta function* (see [1] for a good introduction to this rather complicated function) in conjunction with an area of mathematics called *complex function theory*. Proofs of the prime number theorem making use of these techniques are called 'analytic'.

Mathematicians then searched for a proof of the theorem that was arithmetic in nature and would not need to use the properties of the zeta function or techniques from complex analysis. Such proofs are called 'elementary', although we note here that this word is used in a technical sense; it most certainly does not mean that the proof will necessarily be simple! Both the Norwegian mathematician Atle Selberg and the Hungarian mathematician Paul Erdös devised elementary proofs at around the same time. It is unfortunate, however, that the history of the publication of the proof was somewhat mired in controversy. This is because Selberg went ahead and published in 1949 without in any way acknowledging the contribution from Erdös. Selberg, as a consequence, took the bulk of the credit and was awarded the Fields Medal for his work. (A Fields Medal is the nearest you can get to a Nobel Prize in Mathematics.) Note that a version of Selberg's proof can be found in [11].

Challenge 19.1 Use the prime number theorem to show that the proportion of primes in the first n terms of any arithmetic progression tends to 0 as $n \to \infty$. In other words, prove that the density of primes in any arithmetic progression is 0. (Incidentally, a third way of putting this is that 'almost all' numbers in an arithmetic progression are composite, where the phrase 'almost all' is used in a relative sense.)

---

5. A slightly less daunting undertaking than the prime number theorem might be the investigation and proof of Chebyshev's bounds for $\pi(x)$. The Russian mathematician Pafnuty Chebyshev, mentioned briefly in chapter 1, showed in 1850 that, for $n \geq 2$,

$$\frac{n}{8 \log n} < \pi(x) < \frac{6n}{\log n}.$$

As can be seen, this result might be regarded as a somewhat weaker version of the prime number theorem. It is actually remarkably easy to prove, relatively speaking; certainly far more straightforward than Dirichlet's theorem. A detailed proof is given in [6].

Another interesting result is Bertrand's postulate, which states that for any $n \in \mathbb{N}$ there always exists a prime p such that $n < p \leq 2n$.

It was named after the French Mathematician, Josef Bertrand (1822–1900), who conjectured it in 1845. It should not actually be called a postulate anymore since it was proved by Chebyshev, again in 1850. See [6] for a reasonably transparent proof of this result.

6. In chapter 1 we showed that Dirichlet's theorem is true for the special case $\{4n+3\}$. A number of other special cases can also be proved relatively easily. The progression $\{4n+1\}$ is covered in [1], for example. This utilises a result from number theory sometimes referred to as the *Euler-Fermat theorem* or simply *Euler's theorem*. It can also be shown, without too much difficulty, that there are infinitely primes of the form $8n+7$, but this requires more mathematical machinery still, namely the theory of *quadratic residues* of primes. A proof of this result is given in [4]. Note that it implies that there are infinitely primes of the form $2n+1$ and of the form $4n+3$.

We next look at a slightly more general result that might be thought to lie between Dirichlet's theorem and the results given above.

7. Consider the solution $\omega = \cos\frac{2\pi}{n} + i\sin\frac{2\pi}{n}$ of the equation $x^n = 1$. As discussed in chapter 7, ω is one of the nth roots of unity, and it has order n. Note that ω^k also has order n whenever $\gcd(n,k) = 1$. These $\phi(n)$ elements are each generators of the cyclic group $(G_n, \times)$ from chapter 7. It turns out that the polynomial

$$\prod_{\gcd(n,k)=1} \left(x - \omega^k\right)$$

has integer coefficients; it is called a *cyclotomic polynomial*. For example, with $n = 3$ we have

$$\prod_{\gcd(n,k)=1} \left(x - \omega^k\right) = \prod_{\gcd(3,k)=1} \left(x - \omega^k\right)$$
$$= (x - \omega)\left(x - \omega^2\right)$$
$$= x^2 + x + 1.$$

You might like to check that the cyclotomic polynomial corresponding to the 4th roots of unity is $x^2 + 1$.

The relevance of cyclotomic polynomials to this book is that they can be used to prove that, for any $k \in \mathbb{N}$, the sequence $\{kn+1\}$ contains infinitely many primes. This is the special case of Dirichlet's theorem for which $b = 1$; see [17]. It should be of no great surprise, therefore, to find that these polynomials are intimately associated with both Euler's phi function and the Möbius function, and further details may be found online at [23].

8. Another highly ambitious target would be to work towards an understanding of an analytic proof of Dirichlet's theorem. This would require a detailed study of various aspects of complex analysis, including, as for the prime number theorem, knowledge of properties of the zeta and related functions. For example, see [14, 19, 20], each of which gives a slightly different analytic proof.

9. If you are interested in doing a little more reading in connection with the mathematics of prime numbers then I can recommend any of [1, 4, 8, 11].

10. Finally, although I hope you have enjoyed the proof of Dirichlet's theorem for its own sake, let me just give you a flavour of some of its applications in other areas of number theory.
    (a) Dirichlet's theorem can be put to use in the proof of the 'three squares' theorem [11], which states that

    > A positive integer can be expressed as the sum of three squares if, and only if, it is not of the form $4^m(8n + 7)$ for some non-negative integers m and n.

    (b) Dirichlet's theorem also implies

    > For any fixed $n \in \mathbb{N}$ there are infinitely many primes p such that
    > $$|p - q| > n$$
    > whenever q is a prime not equal to p.

    (c) Dirichlet's theorem has also been employed in more advanced areas of number theory; for example, to help derive *Hasse's Principle* and to solve problems associated with *elliptic curves*. You can read about these in [11].

Challenge 19.2   I will leave you with the following two problems.

(a) With the assistance of Dirichlet's theorem, prove the statement given in 10(b) on the facing page. Half the battle here lies in understanding exactly what this statement is claiming! What it is saying essentially is that for any $n \in \mathbb{N}$ you give me, I will be able to find infinitely many primes such that for each of them the gap to the nearest prime (in either direction) exceeds n.

(b) Prove that Dirichlet's theorem is equivalent to the statement:

Let $b \in \mathbb{N}$ be fixed. For each $a \in \mathbb{N}$ satisfying $\gcd(a,b) = 1$ there exists some $n \in \mathbb{N}$ such that $an + b$ is prime.

Appendices

Appendix A

Convergent sequences and series

The concepts of *convergence* and *divergence* are central to much of the work carried out in this book. It is thus important that we define them rigorously. Consider, for example, the sequence $\{u_n\}$ given by

$$\frac{1}{3}, \frac{4}{9}, \frac{13}{27}, \frac{40}{81}, \frac{121}{243}, \ldots \quad \text{(A.1)}$$

This sequence appears to be 'heading' towards $\frac{1}{2}$ in some manner, but what do we really mean by this in a mathematically precise sense?

In words, the sequence (A.1) converges to $\frac{1}{2}$ if for any positive value of ϵ you care to choose, I will be able to find a positive integer N such that u_n is within ϵ of $\frac{1}{2}$ for all values of n greater than N. This may be expressed more concisely as:

This sequence converges to $\frac{1}{2}$ if for any given $\epsilon > 0$ there exists some $N \in \mathbb{N}$ such that

$$\left| u_n - \frac{1}{2} \right| < \epsilon$$

for all $n > N$.

Let us now show that the sequence (A.1) does indeed satisfy this criterion and is thus a convergent sequence. Note that

$$u_n = \frac{3^n - 1}{2 \times 3^n}$$

$$= \frac{1}{2} - \frac{1}{2 \times 3^n},$$

and thus

$$\left| u_n - \frac{1}{2} \right| = \frac{1}{2 \times 3^n}.$$

For any $\epsilon > 0$ the above would be satisfied when

$$\frac{1}{2 \times 3^n} < \epsilon,$$

or, in other words, when

$$n > \frac{-\log(2\epsilon)}{\log 3}.$$

This is sufficient to show that sequence (A.1) converges to $\frac{1}{2}$.

More generally, we have the following definition of a convergent sequence with *limit* $c \in \mathbb{R}$.

Definition A.1 *The sequence* $\{u_n\}$ *converges to* $c \in \mathbb{R}$ *if, for any given* $\epsilon > 0$, *there exists some* $N \in \mathbb{N}$ *such that* $|u_n - c| < \epsilon$ *for all* $n > N$.

This is actually equivalent to the *Cauchy convergence criterion* used in chapter 10, which states that a sequence $\{u_n\}$ converges if, and only if, for any positive number ϵ we can find a number N such that $|u_p - u_q| < \epsilon$ for all $p, q \geq N$. (A sequence with this property is termed a *Cauchy sequence*.) We prove this equivalence here, and will need the notions of *monotone* sequences and *bounded* sequences. The importance of the Cauchy criterion lies in the fact that should a sequence satisfy it then we are able to state that this sequence converges without having to know the limit of the sequence in advance.

Let us first show that any sequence $\{a_n\}$ contains a monotone subsequence $\{a_{n_k}\}$, which is a subsequence of $\{a_n\}$ such that either $a_{n_1} \geq a_{n_2} \geq a_{n_3} \geq \ldots$ or $a_{n_1} \leq a_{n_2} \leq a_{n_3} \leq \ldots$. We define a_{m_k} to be a 'peak' term of $\{a_n\}$ if $a_{m_k} \geq a_i$ for all $i \geq m_k$. Then there are either infinitely many peak terms $a_{m_1}, a_{m_2}, a_{m_3}, \ldots$, in which case we have, by definition, the subsequence $a_{m_1} \geq a_{m_2} \geq a_{m_3} \geq \ldots$, or there are only finitely many

Appendix A: Convergent sequences and series

peak terms, in which case there exists an infinite subsequence satisfying $a_{i_1} < a_{i_2} < a_{i_3} < \cdots$.

The sequence $\{b_n\}$ is bounded if there exists some positive real number M such that $|b_n| < M$ for each $n \in \mathbb{N}$. We now prove that every Cauchy sequence $\{u_n\}$ is bounded. From the definition of a Cauchy sequence, for any given $\epsilon > 0$ there exists some $N \in \mathbb{N}$ such that $|u_p - u_q| < \epsilon$ for all $p, q \geq N$. In particular, it follows from this that $|u_n| < |u_N| + \epsilon$ for all $n \geq N$. Therefore,

$$|u_n| \leq \max\{|u_1|, |u_2|, |u_3|, \ldots, |u_{N-1}|, |u_N| + \epsilon\}$$

for all $n \in \mathbb{N}$, as required.

Next we show that bounded monotone sequences converge. Suppose that the terms of the sequence $\{c_n\}$ satisfy $c_1 \leq c_2 \leq \cdots$, and that there exists some positive real number M such that $|c_n| \leq M$ for all $n \in \mathbb{N}$. Then by the completeness axiom for the real numbers [3, 7], there exists some least upper bound, M_0 say, for the set of numbers appearing in $\{c_n\}$. For any given $\epsilon > 0$, $M_0 - \epsilon$ cannot be an upper bound for $\{c_n\}$. There thus exists some $N \in \mathbb{N}$ such that $c_N > M_0 - \epsilon$. Also, since $\{c_n\}$ is monotonic increasing, $c_n > M_0 - \epsilon$ for all $n \geq N$. Since $c_n \leq M_0$, by the definition of M_0, it follows that $|c_n - M_0| < \epsilon$ for all $n \geq N$. This shows that $\{c_n\}$ converges to M_0. A similar argument can be used to obtain the corresponding result when the terms of $\{c_n\}$ satisfy $c_1 \geq c_2 \geq \cdots$ (in which case the completeness axiom for the real numbers tells us that the set of numbers appearing in $\{c_n\}$ possesses a greatest lower bound).

We may now prove the Cauchy convergence criterion. Suppose first that $\{u_n\}$ converges to c. Then there exists some $N \in \mathbb{N}$ such that $|u_n - c| < \frac{\epsilon}{2}$ for all $n > N$. Therefore

$$\begin{aligned}|u_p - u_q| &= |(u_p - c) + (c - u_q)| \\ &< |u_p - c| + |c - u_q| \\ &< \frac{\epsilon}{2} + \frac{\epsilon}{2} \\ &= \epsilon\end{aligned}$$

for all $p, q > N$. Note that we have made use of the triangle inequality here; see challenge 7.2 on page 56.

Suppose next that $\{u_n\}$ is a sequence for which the criterion holds. We have already shown both that every sequence possesses a monotone subsequence and that every Cauchy sequence is bounded. Since bounded monotone sequences converge, it follows that every Cauchy sequence has a convergent subsequence. Suppose, therefore, that $\{u_n\}$ possesses the subsequence $\{u_{n_i}\}$ with limit c'. We will show that $\{u_n\}$ also converges to c'. Choose M_1 and M_2 such that $|u_p - u_q| < \frac{\epsilon}{2}$ for all $p, q \geq M_1$ and $|u_{n_i} - c'| < \frac{\epsilon}{2}$ for all $n_i > M_2$, respectively. Thus, for all $n > M_1$ and (fixed) $n_i > \max(M_1, M_2)$ it follows that

$$\begin{aligned}|u_n - c'| &= |(u_n - u_{n_i}) + (u_{n_i} - c')| \\ &< |u_n - u_{n_i}| + |u_{n_i} - c'| \\ &< \frac{\epsilon}{2} + \frac{\epsilon}{2} \\ &= \epsilon,\end{aligned}$$

thereby proving the criterion.

A *divergent* sequence is one that is not convergent. So, for example, the sequences

$$5, 8, 11, 14, \ldots \quad \text{and} \quad 1, -1, 1, -1, \ldots,$$

with nth terms $3n + 2$ and $(-1)^{n+1}$, respectively, both diverge. This is because there exists no constant c such that the terms of the sequence $\{3n + 2\}$ satisfy the criterion specified in definition A.1, and similarly for $\{(-1)^{n+1}\}$.

You might like to consider the behaviour of the three sequences whose nth terms are

$$\frac{\sin n}{n}, \quad \frac{2n + (-1)^n}{n} \quad \text{and} \quad \frac{n}{(\log n)^2}.$$

The first and second converge to 0 and 2, respectively, while the last diverges to infinity. It would be a good idea to obtain these results formally, using definition A.1.

Returning to our initial sequence, note that u_n may be written as the sum of the series

$$u_n = \frac{1}{3} + \frac{1}{9} + \frac{1}{27} + \ldots + \frac{1}{3^n},$$

so it does in fact make sense to say that the sum of this series converges. We use the notation

$$\sum_{n=1}^{\infty} \frac{1}{3^n}$$

Appendix A: Convergent sequences and series

to denote both the infinite series and, if the series converges, the value of its limiting sum. In this case the series does converge, and we may write

$$\sum_{n=1}^{\infty} \frac{1}{3^n} = \lim_{k \to \infty} \sum_{n=1}^{k} \frac{1}{3^n} = \frac{1}{2}.$$

Issues of convergence in this book will often be couched in terms of series.

One important series that occurs in the solution to question 6 in exercise 5 (see page 40) is the *exponential series*

$$e^x = 1 + x + \frac{x^2}{2!} + \frac{x^3}{3!} + \cdots,$$

which is valid for all $x \in \mathbb{R}$.

If all the terms of the sequence $\{a_n\}$ are positive then there are only two possibilities for $\sum_{n=1}^{\infty} a_n$. Either the partial sums are bounded, in which case the series converges, or the partial sums are unbounded, in which case the series diverges to infinity. It is also possible to consider the behaviour of series whose terms may be complex. The series $\sum_{n=1}^{\infty} z_n$, where $z_n = a_n + ib_n$, converges if, and only if, both $\sum_{n=1}^{\infty} a_n$ and $\sum_{n=1}^{\infty} b_n$ converge.

Note that for a sequence to be convergent (with limit c say) it is not necessary that all the terms of the sequence are different from c. The sequence

$$1, 1, 1, 1, \ldots$$

with nth term equal to 1 does indeed converge to 1. Also, some think that the terms of a divergent sequence have to shoot off to infinity. Although the partial sums of many well-known divergent series (such as the *harmonic series*; see chapter 3) do behave in this manner, it does not have to be the case. So long as the sequence does not converge then it is said to diverge.

Appendix B

Proof by contradiction

A classic and simple application of proof by contradiction is with regard to showing that $\sqrt{2}$ is irrational. The idea is to assume that $\sqrt{2}$ is in fact rational, and subsequently to demonstrate that this assumption leads to mathematical nonsense (the contradiction). This in turn would imply that the assumption was false, and hence that $\sqrt{2}$ is indeed irrational.

Theorem B.1 *The number $\sqrt{2}$ is irrational.*

PROOF Suppose that $\sqrt{2}$ is rational. Then we may write

$$\sqrt{2} = \frac{m}{n}$$

for some positive integers m and n with no prime factors in common; this just means that the fraction $\frac{m}{n}$ is in fully-simplified form. On squaring both sides and rearranging, we obtain

$$m^2 = 2n^2. \qquad (B.1)$$

By the Fundamental Theorem of Arithmetic (see theorem 2.1 on page 12) each of m and n may be written uniquely as a product of primes. In particular, let a and b be the exponents of 2 in the prime factorisations of m and n respectively. Note that a or b could be zero; if $a = 0$ then 2 does not appear in the prime factorisation of m, and similarly for b and n. The exponents of 2 in m^2 and $2n^2$ are thus $2a$ and $2b + 1$ respectively. Then, from result (B.1) and theorem 2.1 it follows that $2a = 2b + 1$. However, since both a and b are integers, this cannot be true. We have thus arrived at a contradiction, which tells us that the initial assumption concerning the rationality of $\sqrt{2}$ must be false. ❑

A nice challenge is to adapt the above proof in order to show that $\sqrt{n}$ is irrational for any $n \in \mathbb{N}$ that is not a perfect square, or indeed that $\sqrt[k]{n}$ is irrational for any $n \in \mathbb{N}$ that is not a perfect kth power. Although you will encounter far more subtle uses of contradiction in this book, the underlying idea remains the same.

Appendix C

Modular arithmetic

In order to follow certain parts of the proof of Dirichlet's theorem given in this book, it is necessary know something about *modular arithmetic*. Some may already have met this concept whilst studying group theory in further mathematics lessons or maybe even in a first-year undergraduate course on number theory. When one positive integer is divided by another the answer can be given as a *quotient* and a *remainder*. For example, if 34 is divided by 7 then, since $34 = 4 \times 7 + 6$, the quotient is 4 and the remainder is 6. When dividing whole numbers by 7 it is an accepted convention that the remainder will be an integer from the set $\{0, 1, 2, 3, 4, 5, 6\}$, and this generalises in an obvious way when dividing by k.

In connection with this, we will occasionally say that $m \in \mathbb{N}$ is 'reduced modulo k'. This means that m is to be represented by the unique integer from the set $\{0, 1, 2, 3, \ldots, k-1\}$ that is the remainder when it is divided by k. For example, 34 reduced modulo 7 is 6.

If two positive integers m and n leave the same remainder when divided by the positive integer k then they may, in some sense, be regarded as equivalent with respect to k. In this case m and n are said to be *congruent modulo k*, and this is generally written as

$$m \equiv n \pmod{k}.$$

Following on from the previous example, both 34 and 55 leave remainder 6 when divided by 7 so we may write $34 \equiv 55 \equiv 6 \pmod{7}$. Note that if $m \equiv n \pmod{k}$ then it must be true that $m - n = rk$ for some integer r. In other words, $m \equiv n \pmod{k}$ means the difference between m and n is a multiple of k. Such arithmetic is called *modular arithmetic*.

We need to be careful to avoid getting caught out when performing calculations using modular arithmetic. For example, if $k, l, m, n \in \mathbb{N}$ are such that $lm \equiv ln \pmod{k}$, is it necessarily true that $m \equiv n \pmod{k}$? You should very quickly be able to show that it is not. For example, while $12 \times 4 \equiv 12 \times 7 \pmod{18}$ it is certainly not true that 4 is congruent to 7 modulo 18. So it is not just a case of cancelling indiscriminately, as can be done in 'normal' integer arithmetic. However, if $\gcd(18, l) = 1$ then $lm \equiv ln \pmod{18}$ does indeed imply that $m \equiv n \pmod{18}$. To take an example, $5m \equiv 5n \pmod{18}$ implies that $m \equiv n \pmod{18}$. Thus the coprimality of l and 18 may be regarded as a condition that allows cancellation to be carried out whenever $lm \equiv ln \pmod{18}$. The following theorem generalises this modular-arithmetic cancelling law.

Theorem C.1 *Suppose that* $lm \equiv ln \pmod{k}$ *and* $\gcd(k, l) = 1$. *Then* $m \equiv n \pmod{k}$.

PROOF The condition $lm \equiv ln \pmod{k}$ implies that $l(m - n) = rk$ for some integer r. Then, since $\gcd(k, l) = 1$, it must be true that k divides $m - n$. We may therefore write $m - n = tk$ for some integer t, from which it follows that $m \equiv n \pmod{k}$. ❏

There are exactly $\phi(k)$ numbers in the set $\{1, 2, 3, \ldots, k\}$ that are coprime to k, where ϕ is Euler's phi function; see definition 4.2 on page 29. Labelling these as $a_1, a_2, a_3, \ldots, a_{\phi(k)}$, we now prove a result concerning the product of each of these numbers with m, where $\gcd(k, m) = 1$. Note that the set $\{a_1, a_2, a_3, \ldots, a_{\phi(k)}\}$ is denoted by R_k in definition 6.3 on page 48, a notation that is used from that point on.

Theorem C.2 *If* $\gcd(k, m) = 1$ *then* $ma_1, ma_2, ma_3, \ldots, ma_{\phi(k)}$ *are congruent modulo* k *to* $a_1, a_2, a_3, \ldots, a_{\phi(k)}$ *in some order*.

PROOF Suppose that $ma_i \equiv ma_j \pmod{k}$ but $a_i \neq a_j$. Since $\gcd(k, m) = 1$, we may, by theorem C.1, cancel the ms to obtain $a_i \equiv a_j \pmod{k}$, which implies $a_i = a_j$, a contradiction. Thus each of $ma_1, ma_2, ma_3, \ldots, ma_{\phi(k)}$ is distinct modulo k. Note also that when any of these numbers is reduced modulo k it will also be coprime to k, and will thus be an element of the set $R_k = \{a_1, a_2, a_3, \ldots, a_{\phi(k)}\}$. This is enough to prove the theorem. ❏

Theorem C.2 implies, since $1 \in R_k$, that if $\gcd(k, m) = 1$ then there exists some $r \in R_k$ such that $rm \equiv 1 \pmod{k}$. The integer r is known as a *multiplicative inverse* of m modulo k. This is equivalent to saying that if m and k are coprime then there exist integers r and s such that $rm + sk = 1$.

Appendix D

Complex numbers

We provide here some simple definitions and results concerning complex numbers that will be required when studying the mathematics associated with Dirichlet characters in chapter 9. This also complements some of the material on nth roots of unity that is introduced in chapter 7. First, it is necessary to introduce the notion of the complex conjugate of a complex number.

Definition D.1 *If $z = a + bi$ for some $a, b \in \mathbb{R}$ then $\bar{z} = a - bi$ is known as the* complex conjugate *of z.*

From this definition it follows that

$$z\bar{z} = (a+bi)(a-bi) = a^2 - abi + bai - bi^2$$
$$= a^2 + b^2.$$

The product of a number with its complex conjugate is thus always a real number.

To highlight another property of the complex conjugate, let $z_1 = a + bi$ and $z_2 = c + di$. Then

$$\bar{z}_1 \bar{z}_2 = (a-bi)(c-di)$$
$$= (ac - bd) - i(ad + bc),$$

and

$$\overline{z_1 z_2} = \overline{(ac - bd) + i(ad + bc)}$$
$$= (ac - bd) - i(ad + bc),$$

which shows that $\overline{z_1 \overline{z}_2} = \overline{z_1} z_2$.

An application of this result appears in the proof of the fact that the non-real roots of any polynomial with real coefficients always come in conjugate pairs, as follows. Let $f(z) = a_0 + a_1 z + \cdots + a_n z^n$ be a polynomial in z of degree n such that $a_0, a_1, \ldots, a_n \in \mathbb{R}$. Suppose that α is a root of $f(z) = 0$. Then $a_0 + a_1 \alpha + \cdots + a_n \alpha^n = 0$, and hence

$$\begin{aligned} 0 &= \overline{a_0 + a_1 \alpha + \cdots + a_n \alpha^n} \\ &= \overline{a_0} + \overline{a_1 \alpha} + \cdots + \overline{a_n \alpha^n} \\ &= \overline{a_0} + \overline{a_1}\,\overline{\alpha} + \cdots + \overline{a_n}\,\overline{\alpha}^z \\ &= a_0 + a_1 \overline{\alpha} + \cdots + a_n \overline{\alpha}^n, \end{aligned}$$

which shows that $\overline{\alpha}$ is also a root of $f(z) = 0$. In particular, this property can clearly be seen in figure 7.1 on page 54 for the the polynomial $f(z) = z^6 - 1$.

The concept of the *modulus* of a complex number z will also be needed. This is written $|z|$, and might be regarded as the 'length' or 'size' of z.

Definition D.2 *Let $z = a + bi \in \mathbb{C}$. The modulus of z is given by*

$$|z| = \sqrt{a^2 + b^2}.$$

To take an example, if $z = 6 - 4i$ then

$$\begin{aligned} |z| &= \sqrt{6^2 + 4^2} \\ &= \sqrt{52} \\ &= 2\sqrt{13}. \end{aligned}$$

When a complex number z is written as $a + bi$ we say that it is in *Cartesian form*. This is indeed the way of representing complex numbers that most of us will have encountered first. In many situations, however, they may be more conveniently expressed in *modulus-argument form*. This essentially locates a complex number z on an Argand diagram via polar coordinates, with the modulus being the distance from the origin and the *argument* being the angle between the positive x axis and the line connecting z to the origin. By convention, the argument θ is given in radians and satisfies $-\pi < \theta \leq \pi$. For example, $z_1 = 1 + i$ has modulus $\sqrt{2}$ and argument $\frac{\pi}{4}$, while $z_2 = 1 - i\sqrt{3}$ has modulus 2 and argument $-\frac{\pi}{3}$. Note that we may write

$$z_1 = \sqrt{2}\left(\cos\left(\frac{\pi}{4}\right) + i \sin\left(\frac{\pi}{4}\right)\right)$$

and
$$z_2 = 2\left(\cos\left(-\frac{\pi}{3}\right) + i\sin\left(-\frac{\pi}{3}\right)\right).$$
A well-known result, readily proved by induction, is given by
$$(\cos\theta + i\sin\theta)^n = \cos n\theta + i\sin n\theta$$
for integer n. This is known as *De Moivre's theorem*.

Appendix E

Double sums

Much of the material in the later parts of this book requires facility with double sums. These are used to denote sums of expressions possessing two indices of summation subject to various conditions on the integer values these indices are allowed to take. Here is a simple example to get us started:

$$\sum_{k=1}^{2} \sum_{n=1}^{3} (5k - n) = (5 \times 1 - 1) + (5 \times 1 - 2) + (5 \times 1 - 3)$$
$$+ (5 \times 2 - 1) + (5 \times 2 - 2) + (5 \times 2 - 3)$$
$$= 33.$$

This evaluation was carried out by holding the value of k fixed at 1 on the outer sum whilst running through the values of n on the inner sum, and then doing a similar thing for $k = 2$. The region of summation may be seen in figure E.1.

Note, however, that this could also have been carried out by holding n fixed at 1 whilst running through the values of k, and so on. Therefore

$$\sum_{k=1}^{2} \sum_{n=1}^{3} (5k - n) = \sum_{n=1}^{3} \sum_{k=1}^{2} (5k - n).$$

This is known as *interchanging the order of summation*, and is a common operation on double sums.

It is important to realise that interchanging the order of summation is not always simply a matter of swapping over the summation signs. For

Figure E.1

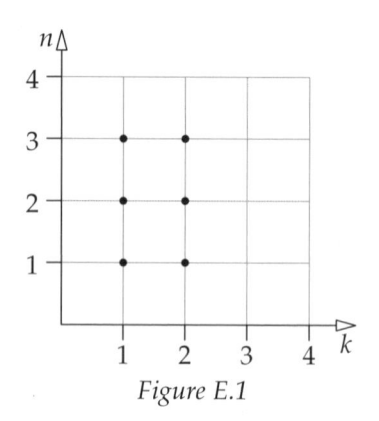

example, on interchanging the order of summation of

$$\sum_{k=1}^{3} \sum_{n=1}^{k} (2k+n)^2,$$

in which the index on the inner sum is restricted by the current value of the index on the outer sum, we obtain

$$\sum_{n=1}^{3} \sum_{k=n}^{3} (2k+n)^2,$$

as you should indeed check. The region of summation for this particular case may be seen in figure E.2. This result can be generalised.

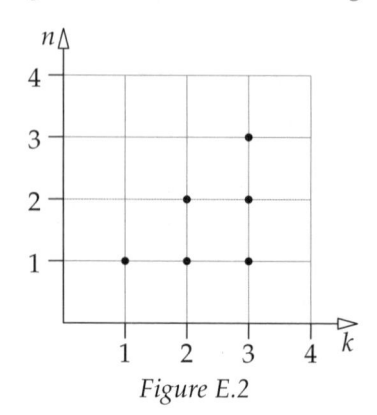

Figure E.2

A particularly simple situation arises when the expression under the double sum is separable into the product of two functions, one containing only the index k and the other only n. For example,

$$\sum_{k=2}^{5} \sum_{n=1}^{3} \left(k + kn^2\right) = \sum_{k=2}^{5} \left(k \sum_{n=1}^{3} (1 + n^2) \right)$$
$$= \left(\sum_{k=2}^{5} k \right) \left(\sum_{n=1}^{3} (1 + n^2) \right)$$
$$= (2 + 3 + 4 + 5)(2 + 5 + 10)$$
$$= 238.$$

In this book we also meet double sums similar to, though generally a little more complicated than,

$$\sum_{p \leq x} \sum_{k=1}^{\infty} \frac{1}{p^k}.$$

The notation on the outer sum signifies that it ranges over all primes less than $x \in \mathbb{R}$. This sum is thus a function of x. To take an example, we have

$$\sum_{p \leq \sqrt{10}} \sum_{k=1}^{\infty} \frac{1}{p^k} = \sum_{k=1}^{\infty} \frac{1}{2^k} + \sum_{k=1}^{\infty} \frac{1}{3^k}$$
$$= 1 + \tfrac{1}{2}$$
$$= \tfrac{3}{2},$$

on using the formula for the sum to infinity of a geometric progression.

Finally, we look at double sums for which the indices range over the factors of various numbers; these are first encountered in chapter 11. The sum

$$\sum_{d|n} \sum_{k|\frac{n}{d}} f(d) g(k)$$

for two arithmetic functions f and g is actually a function of n. The outer sum ranges over all factors d of n while, for a fixed value of d, the inner sum ranges over all factors of $\frac{n}{d}$. So if $n = 4$ this double sum is equal to

$$f(1)(g(1) + g(2) + g(4)) + f(2)(g(1) + g(2)) + f(4)g(1).$$

In challenge 11.2 on page 86 you are asked to prove a result that implies that

$$\sum_{d|n} \sum_{k|\frac{n}{d}} f(d) g(k) = \sum_{k|n} \sum_{d|\frac{n}{k}} f(d) g(k).$$

Notation

$\mathbb{N}$	Set of positive integers.
$\mathbb{Z}$	Set of integers.
$\mathbb{Q}$	Set of rational numbers.
$\mathbb{R}$	Set of real numbers.
$\mathbb{C}$	Set of complex numbers.
$\mathbb{R}\setminus\{0\}$	Set of non-zero real numbers.
$x \in \mathbb{R}$	x is a real number.
$A\setminus B$	The difference between sets A and B.
$\{a_n\}$	Sequence with nth term a_n.
$m \mid n$	m is a factor of n.
$m \nmid n$	m is not a factor of n.
$m \equiv n \pmod{k}$	m is congruent to n modulo k.
$m \not\equiv n \pmod{k}$	m is not congruent to n modulo k.
$\gcd(m,n)$	Greatest common divisor (or highest common factor) of m and n.
$n!$	n factorial; $1 \times 2 \times 3 \times \cdots \times n$.
$\lfloor x \rfloor$	Floor function.
$\binom{n}{k}$	Binomial coefficient.
$\exp x$	An alternative notation to e^x.
$\log x$	In this book, $\log x$ will always denote $\log_e x$ or $\ln x$.
$\lvert z \rvert$	Modulus of z.
$\bar{z}$	Complex conjugate of z.

$A \Rightarrow B$	A implies B.
$A \Leftrightarrow B$	A if, and only if, B.
$(R_k, \otimes_k)$	The group of numbers from the set $\{1, 2, \ldots, k\}$ that are coprime to k under $\otimes_k$, multiplication modulo k.
$\mu(n)$	Möbius function.
$\Lambda(n)$	Mangoldt function.
$\phi(n)$	Euler's phi function.
$\pi(x)$	Number of primes not exceeding x.
$\chi_f(n)$	Dirichlet character.
$f * g$	Dirichlet product of f and g.
$f \circ G$	Generalised convolution of f and G.
$\sum_{d\mid n} f(d)$	The arithmetic function f summed over all factors d of n.
$\sum_{n \leq x} f(n)$	f summed over all $n \in \mathbb{N}$ not exceeding $x \in \mathbb{R}$.
$\sum_{p \leq x} f(p)$	f summed over all primes p not exceeding $x \in \mathbb{R}$.
$\prod_p f(p)$	The infinite product over the primes given by

$$f(2)f(3)f(5)\cdots.$$

Hints to the challenges

Challenge 1.1

Suppose that a and b are both positive integers. You may have noticed straight away that if $b \geq 2$ then setting $n = b$ gives the term $ab + b = b(a + 1)$, which is composite (in other words, not prime). Can we find a similar method that covers all cases, and shows that it is never possible for *all* the terms in the arithmetic progression given by $\{an + b : n = 0, 1, 2, \ldots\}$ to be prime? Well, on setting $n = a + b + 1$ gives $an + b = a^2 + ab + a + b = (a+b)(a+1)$.

Challenge 2.1

Let k be the total number of distinct prime factors appearing in the prime factorisations of either m or n. Then for some set of primes $\{p_1, p_2, \ldots, p_k\}$ we can write

$$m = p_1^{a_1} p_2^{a_2} \cdots p_k^{a_k} \quad \text{and} \quad n = p_1^{b_1} p_2^{b_2} \cdots p_k^{b_k},$$

where some of the exponents may be zero.
(a) With $c_i = \min\{a_i, b_i\}$ then $\gcd(m, n) = p_1^{c_1} p_2^{c_2} \cdots p_k^{c_k}$.
(b) Use the max function.
(c) Think about how you might use your answers to (a) and (b) in order to prove this.
(d) This question is really asking for the number of factors of $\gcd(m, n)$. As a hint, you might want to have a quick glance at chapter 4.
(e) This essentially boils down to listing the possible combinations of exponents in a systematic manner.

Challenge 3.1

Notice first that the line $y = x + 1$ is tangential to the curve $y = e^x$ when $x = 0$. Now complete the argument by showing that the gradient of $y = e^x$ is greater than that of $y = x + 1$ for any $x > 0$ but that the reverse is true for any $x < 0$.

Challenge 4.1

Using the initial hints given in this challenge you will soon obtain the result
$$\sigma(p^k) = \frac{p^{k+1} - 1}{p - 1}.$$
See if you can build on this to obtain a more general formula.

Challenge 4.2

Suppose that it is not the case that $f(n) = 0$ for all positive integers n. Then there exists some integer m such that $f(m) \neq 0$. Since $\gcd(m, 1) = 1$ and f is multiplicative, we have $f(m) = f(m \times 1) = f(m)f(1)$. Then, as $f(m) \neq 0$, we may cancel $f(m)$ from both sides of the equation to give $f(1) = 1$, as required.

Challenge 4.3

Let p be a prime. Then, for any $k \in \mathbb{N}$, $\gcd(p^k, n) = 1$ if, and only if, p is not a factor of n. The only integers in the set $\{1, 2, \ldots, p^k\}$ that have p as a factor are the p^{k-1} numbers $p, 2p, \ldots, p^k$. From this it follows that $\phi(p^k) = p^k - p^{k-1}$. You might next like to provide an argument for the fact that $\phi(pq) = (p-1)(q-1)$ for any distinct primes p and q, and proceed from there. For a proof of (b) that does not use (a), see [4].

Challenge 5.1

On expanding the left-hand side, the dominant term is $81x^4$. It is then a matter of showing that the remaining terms may be 'swallowed up' by the x^3 term. Note in particular, from challenge 3.1 on page 20, that $x - 1 > \log x > 0$ for all $x > 1$, which implies that $x^2 \log x = O(x^3)$.

Challenge 5.2

You should convince yourself that all are correct statements except for (d). This should be
$$\frac{1}{x^2} + \frac{2\sin x}{x} = O\left(\frac{1}{x}\right).$$

Challenge 5.3

The inequality may be rewritten as
$$-x \le (1-2t)x + t(t-1) \le x.$$

Since $-1 \le 1-2t \le 1$ and $-\frac{1}{4} \le t(t-1) \le 0$ when $0 \le t \le 1$, then $(1-2t)x + t(t-1) \le x$. Now show that the left-hand inequality is also true, starting from $(1-2t)x + t(t-1) + x = (1-t)(2x-t)$.

Challenge 6.1

First, the sum of the two rational numbers $\frac{a}{b}$ and $\frac{c}{d}$ is $\frac{ad+bc}{bd}$, which is also rational. Addition is associative and 0 (which is itself rational) is the identity. Finally, $\frac{a}{b} + \left(-\frac{a}{b}\right) = 0$, so we have inverses.

It is not true, however, that $\mathbb{Q}$ forms a group with respect to multiplication. To see this, note that 1 is the identity in this case but there exists no rational number x such that $x \times 0 = 1$.

Challenge 6.2

If e_1 and e_2 are identity elements of G, then from the group axioms we have $e_1 = e_1 e_2 = e_2$, which shows that G has a unique identity. In order to show that inverses are unique you might proceed as follows. Let e be the identity of G, and suppose that b_1 and b_2 are inverses of the element a. Then $b_1 = eb_1 = b_2 a b_1 = b_2 e = b_2$.

Challenge 6.3

In preparation for what is to follow, it is worthwhile checking meticulously that all the group axioms are satisfied. So start by checking that the set $\{1, 3, 7, 9\}$ is closed with respect to multiplication modulo 10. For example, $7 \times 9 = 63 \equiv 3 \pmod{10}$. We certainly have associativity, and the identity is 1. Finally, check for inverses. For example, $3 \times 7 = 7 \times 3 = 21 \equiv 1 \pmod{10}$.

Challenge 6.4

A thorough reading of appendix C should be more than enough to set you on your way in this challenge.

Challenge 6.5

The rows and columns of the Cayley table of a finite group G are labelled with the n elements of the group. (We assume that the ordering of the row labels is identical to that of the column labels.) The fact that the entries in the table consist solely of these elements reflects the closure property of the group. The identity axiom means that exactly one row of the table will match the column labels precisely, and the corresponding column will match the row labels precisely. If $e, a \in G$, with e the identity, then, since $aa^{-1} = a^{-1}a = e$, it follows that the identity elements appearing in the table are placed symmetrically about the leading diagonal. On the other hand, it is not so easy to check for the associativity of the binary operation merely by glancing at the table. There is, however, a procedure known as *Light's associativity test* [25] that is reasonably efficient at checking for associativity.

In table 1 we see an example of a 3×3 Latin square that cannot be the Cayley table of a finite group. It is easy to spot that there is no identity. Furthermore, note for example that $a \circ (a \circ b) = a \circ b = b$ while $(a \circ a) \circ b = e \circ b = a$, showing that associativity is not satisfied in general.

∘	e	a	b
e	e	b	a
a	a	e	b
b	b	a	e

Table 1

Challenge 6.6

Since G is finite and closed with respect to the binary operation, it follows that all we need to do is to show that each of the elements in $\{a_1 a, a_2 a, \ldots, a_n a\}$ is distinct. Suppose, therefore, that $a_i a = a_j a$. Then $a_i a a^{-1} = a_j a a^{-1}$ so that $a_i = a_j$, as required. (Notice from this that groups possess a cancellation law.) The same type of argument shows that $G = \{a a_1, a a_2, \ldots, a a_n\}$.

Challenge 7.1

We know that if z is an nth root of unity then it is of the form

$$z = \cos \frac{2\pi k}{n} + i \sin \frac{2\pi k}{n}.$$

Then

$$\begin{aligned} z\bar{z} &= \left(\cos \frac{2\pi k}{n} + i \sin \frac{2\pi k}{n}\right)\left(\cos \frac{2\pi k}{n} - i \sin \frac{2\pi k}{n}\right) \\ &= \cos^2 \frac{2\pi k}{n} + \sin^2 \frac{2\pi k}{n} \\ &= 1. \end{aligned}$$

Challenge 7.2

The modulus $|z|$ of a complex number z is dealt with in appendix D and in the exercises in chapter 7. First, we have

$$\begin{aligned} |z_1 + z_2|^2 &= (z_1 + z_2)\overline{(z_1 + z_2)} \\ &= z_1 \bar{z}_1 + z_1 \bar{z}_2 + z_2 \bar{z}_1 + z_2 \bar{z}_2 \\ &= |z_1|^2 + |z_2|^2 + z_1 \bar{z}_2 + z_2 \bar{z}_1. \end{aligned}$$

Now,

$$\begin{aligned} z_1 \bar{z}_2 + z_2 \bar{z}_1 &= z_1 \bar{z}_2 + \overline{z_1 \bar{z}_2} \\ &= 2 \operatorname{Re}(z_1 \bar{z}_2) \\ &\leq 2 |z_1| |z_2|. \end{aligned}$$

The above results give

$$|z_1 + z_2|^2 \leq |z_1|^2 + |z_2|^2 + 2|z_1||z_2|,$$

and, on taking positive square roots, the triangle inequality follows. Now use induction to prove the generalised result.

Challenge 8.1

Suppose that f is a character of $(R_{15}, \otimes_{15})$. Then, using the information given in the text that $\{2, 14\}$ is a set of generators, and the orders of 2 and 14 are 4 and 2, respectively, we may assign $1, -1, i$ or $-i$ to $f(2)$, and 1 or -1 to $f(14)$. This results in the character table for $(R_{15}, \otimes_{15})$ shown in table 2.

n	$f_1(n)$	$f_2(n)$	$f_3(n)$	$f_4(n)$	$f_5(n)$	$f_6(n)$	$f_7(n)$	$f_8(n)$
1	1	1	1	1	1	1	1	1
2	1	1	−1	−1	i	i	−i	−i
4	1	1	1	1	−1	−1	−1	−1
7	1	−1	−1	1	−i	i	i	−i
8	1	1	−1	−1	−i	−i	i	i
11	1	−1	1	−1	−1	1	−1	1
13	1	−1	−1	1	i	−i	−i	i
14	1	−1	1	−1	1	−1	1	−1

Table 2

Challenge 9.1

First, suppose $n \in \mathbb{N}$ satisfies $\gcd(n, k) = 1$. Then their exists some $\widehat{n} \in \{0, 1, \ldots, k-1\}$ such that $n \equiv \widehat{n} \pmod{k}$. However, this implies that $n + k \equiv \widehat{n} \pmod{k}$, from which we see that $\chi_f(k+n) = f(\widehat{n}) = \chi_f(n)$.

If, on the other hand, $\gcd(n, k) > 1$ then $\gcd(n+k, k) > 1$. In this case we have $\chi_f(n) = \chi_f(n+k) = 0$.

Challenge 9.2

If $m = n$ then

$$\sum_{i=1}^{\phi(k)} f_m(a_i)\overline{f}_n(a_i) = \sum_{i=1}^{\phi(k)} (f_m\overline{f}_m)(a_i)$$

Hints to the challenges

$$= \sum_{i=1}^{\phi(k)} f_1(a_i)$$
$$= \phi(k).$$

On the other hand, if $m \neq n$ then

$$\sum_{i=1}^{\phi(k)} f_m(a_i)\overline{f_n}(a_i) = \sum_{i=1}^{\phi(k)} (f_m\overline{f_n})(a_i)$$
$$= \sum_{i=1}^{\phi(k)} f_j(a_i),$$

for some $j \neq 1$. It follows from result (9.4) that this sum is equal to zero.

Challenge 10.1

The hints already provided should be sufficient in order to evaluate these three integrals. Just make sure you are careful with regard to the algebraic manipulations.

Challenge 10.2

From

$$\sum_{x<n\leq y} \frac{\chi_m(n)}{n} = O\left(\frac{1}{x}\right)$$

we know that there exist some $X, M \in \mathbb{R}$ such that

$$\left|\sum_{x<n\leq y} \frac{\chi_m(n)}{n}\right| < \frac{M}{x}$$

when $x > X$. Thus, for any given $\epsilon > 0$, we have

$$\left|\sum_{x<n\leq y} \frac{\chi_m(n)}{n}\right| < \epsilon$$

when

$$x > \max\left\{X, \frac{M}{\epsilon}\right\}.$$

Now let
$$u_j = \sum_{n=1}^{j} \frac{\chi_m(n)}{n}$$

and $p, q \in \mathbb{N}$ such that, without loss of generality, $p > q$. Then

$$|u_p - u_q| = \left| \sum_{n=q+1}^{p} \frac{\chi_m(n)}{n} \right| < \epsilon$$

when

$$p, q > \max\left\{X, \frac{M}{\epsilon}\right\}.$$

Challenge 10.3

With $A(x)$ as before, and $f(x)$ some arbitrary function on the positive real numbers, then

$$\sum_{x < n \leq y} \chi_m(n)f(n) = \sum_{n=a+1}^{b-1} A(n)(f(n) - f(n+1)) \\ + A(b)f(b) - A(a)f(a+1).$$

Now it is true that

$$\sum_{n=a+1}^{b-1} |A(n)(f(n) - f(n+1))| = \sum_{n=a+1}^{b-1} |A(n)|(f(n) - f(n+1))$$

so long as $f(n) \geq f(n+1)$ for $n = a+1, a+2, \ldots, b-1$, in which case we obtain

$$\sum_{x < n \leq y} \chi_m(n)f(n) = O(f(x)).$$

In chapter 10 we showed that L_m converges (and gave an a asymptotic formula for it) using $f(n) = \frac{1}{n}$, noting that in this case $f(n) > f(n+1)$ for all $n \in \mathbb{N}$. In order to show that

$$L'_m \quad \text{and} \quad \sum_{n=1}^{\infty} \frac{\chi_m(n)}{\sqrt{n}}$$

both converge, set $f(n)$ equal to $\frac{\log n}{n}$ and $\frac{1}{\sqrt{n}}$, respectively, and use the Cauchy convergence criterion once more. The formulae (10.4) and (10.5) follow.

Challenge 11.1

Assume throughout that $\gcd(m,n) = 1$. First, if either $p^2 \mid m$ or $p^2 \mid n$ for some prime p, then $p^2 \mid mn$, showing that $\mu(m)\mu(n) = 0 = \mu(mn)$. Suppose, on the other hand, that $m = p_1 p_2 \cdots p_i$ and $n = q_1 q_2 \cdots q_j$ for primes $p_1, \ldots, p_i, q_1, \ldots, q_j$. The assumption that $\gcd(m,n) = 1$ implies that all the primes in this list are distinct. Therefore, $\mu(m)\mu(n) = (-1)^i(-1)^j = (-1)^{i+j}$ and $\mu(mn) = \mu(p_1 \cdots p_i q_1 \cdots q_j) = (-1)^{i+j}$, as required.

Challenge 11.2

First, $d \mid n$ implies that $\frac{n}{d}$ is an integer so that $k \mid \frac{n}{d}$ does indeed make sense. Then $\frac{n}{d} = ak$, giving $n = adk$. From this we see that $k \mid n$. Also, $ad = \frac{n}{k}$, showing that $d \mid \frac{n}{k}$. Now do a similar thing for the reverse implication.

Challenge 12.1

Let $m, n \in \mathbb{N}$ be such that $\gcd(m,n) = 1$. Note that in this case any factor of mn may be written as $d_1 d_2$ where $d_1 \mid m$ and $d_2 \mid n$. It is clear that

$$\gcd(d_1, d_2) = \gcd\left(\frac{m}{d_1}, \frac{n}{d_2}\right) = 1.$$

By definition 12.1, and using the fact that f and g are both multiplicative, we have

$$h(mn) = \sum_{d \mid n} f(d) g\left(\frac{mn}{d}\right)$$

$$= \sum_{\substack{d_1 \mid m \\ d_2 \mid n}} f(d_1) f(d_2) g\left(\frac{m}{d_1}\right) g\left(\frac{n}{d_2}\right)$$

$$= \sum_{d_1 \mid m} f(d_1) g\left(\frac{m}{d_1}\right) \sum_{d_2 \mid n} f(d_2) g\left(\frac{n}{d_2}\right)$$

$$= h(m) h(n).$$

Challenge 12.2

We are given that

$$G(x) = \sum_{n \le x} f^{-1}(n) H\left(\frac{x}{n}\right),$$

which may be written as $G = f^{-1} \circ H$. Therefore,

$$\begin{aligned} f \circ G &= f \circ (f^{-1} \circ H) \\ &= (f * f^{-1}) \circ H \\ &= I \circ H \\ &= H. \end{aligned}$$

Challenge 12.3

First, let $\alpha(n) = 1$ for all $n \in \mathbb{N}$, noting this this is a completely multiplicative arithmetic function. Next, restrict x to the positive integers. Finally, let F and G be arithmetic functions (we define these functions to be zero for non-integral arguments). Then result (12.3) does in fact give rise to result (11.2). In order to avoid notational confusion, note that G and F in result (12.3) correspond, respectively, to F and f in result (11.2).

Challenge 14.1

Rather than consider the situation for general x initially, it might be an idea to look at a specific example, say $x = 4\frac{1}{2}$. Make a sketch of figure 14.1 and then draw in the vertical line $t = 4\frac{1}{2}$. This will lead to the right-hand inequality of (14.5) for this special case. Similarly, figure 14.1 gives rise to the left-hand inequality of (14.5). You can then generalise.

Challenge 14.2

We may write $\frac{x}{2p}$ as $k + \alpha$ for some integer k and real number α such that $0 \leq \alpha < 1$. Then $2\lfloor \frac{x}{2p} \rfloor = 2k$ and $\lfloor \frac{x}{p} \rfloor$ is equal to either $2k$ or $2k + 1$ according as to whether $0 \leq \alpha < \frac{1}{2}$ or $\frac{1}{2} \leq \alpha < 1$, respectively.

Challenge 16.1

We only need to sum over powers of primes since Mangoldt's function is zero on the composite numbers. The outer sum on the right-hand side of the first line picks out the primes p not exceeding x while the inner one sums, for a particular value of p, over all the powers of p that do not exceed x (the upper limit $c(x, p)$ ensures that the sum is over exactly those not exceeding x). The second line splits the sum up into one that is solely over primes and one that is over higher powers of primes.

Challenge 16.2

In particular, make sure that you understand how the transition from the double to the single sum works. If $f(a,b)$ is a function of the positive integers a and b, then

$$\sum_{n \leq x} \sum_{d \mid n} f(n,d) = \sum_{kd \leq x} f(kd,d),$$

where the sum on the right-hand side is over all ordered pairs (k,d) such that $kd \leq x$. One way of seeing that this is indeed true is to consider the terms that arise on the right-hand side when kd is kept at some fixed value, $n \leq x$ say. We will end up with terms of the form $f(n,d)$ for all d such that $kd = n$ for some $k \in \mathbb{N}$ (in other words, all terms such that $d \mid n$). Also look at how things are rearranged in order to arrive at the alternative double sum in the last line.

Challenge 16.3

This should not cause too many problems, but it is worth going through step by step. For example, where has the $\lfloor x \rfloor$ come from in the second line?

Challenge 19.1

The number of primes in the set $S_n = \{ak + b : k = 0, 1, 2, \ldots, n-1\}$ cannot exceed $\pi(a(n-1)+b)$. The proportion of primes in S_n is therefore no greater than

$$\frac{\pi(a(n-1)+b)}{n}.$$

From the prime number theorem we know that

$$\frac{\pi(a(n-1)+b)}{n} \sim \frac{a(n-1)+b}{n \log(a(n-1)+b)}.$$

However, the expression on the right tends to zero as n tends to infinity, as required.

Challenge 19.2

(a) The integers $(m! - 1)m!$ and $m! + 1$ are coprime for $m \geq 2$. From Dirichlet's theorem it then follows that there are infinitely primes of the form
$$p_k = k(m! - 1)m! + (m! + 1).$$
Note that for any such prime, it is the case that $(i+1) \mid (p_k + i)$ for $1 \leq i \leq m-1$, $m \mid (p_k - 1)$, $(m! - 1) \mid (p_k - 2)$ and $(i-1) \mid (p_k - i)$ for $3 \leq i \leq m+1$. Thus p_k has at least $m+1$ and $m-1$ consecutive composite numbers immediately preceding and immediately following it, respectively.

For any $n \in \mathbb{N}$ there are therefore infinitely primes of the form
$$p_k = k((n+1)! - 1)(n+1)! + ((n+1)! + 1)$$
such that for each of them the gap to the nearest prime (in either direction) exceeds n. For example, the sequence
$$\{14\,280k + 121 : k = 0, 1, 2, \ldots\}$$
contains infinitely many primes for which the gaps to their nearest neighbours exceed 4.

(b) First, it is clear that Dirichlet's theorem implies the statement, so we are left to show that the statement implies Dirichlet's theorem. Let us consider the set $\{an + b : n = 0, 1, 2, \ldots\}$ for some fixed $b \in \mathbb{N}$. The statement says that if $\gcd(a, b) = 1$ there exists some $n_1 \in \mathbb{N}$ and prime p_1 such that $an_1 + b = p_1$. Since $b < p_1$, it must be the case that $\gcd(b, p_1) = 1$ and hence $\gcd(b, ap_1) = 1$. From the statement we then obtain $ap_1 n_2 + b = p_2$ for some $n_2 \in \mathbb{N}$ and prime $p_2 > p_1$, and so on.

Answers and hints to the exercises

Exercise 2

1. (a) $2^4 \times 5^4$;
   (b) $2^3 \times 7^2 \times 11 \times 23$;
   (c) $3^9 \times 5^{18}$;
   (d) $2^{18} \times 3^9 \times 5^4 \times 7^3 \times 11 \times 13 \times 17 \times 19$.

2. It does indeed follow that $p^n \mid m^n$ since $p \mid m^n$ implies that $p \mid m$.

3. (a) Note that $n^2 - 1 = (n+1)(n-1)$, which is composite for $n \geq 3$.
   (b) This follows since $n^3 - 1 = (n-1)(n^2 + n + 1)$.

4. It is not true that $p(n) + 1$ is prime for all $n \in \mathbb{N}$. See if you can find the smallest positive integer n for which $p(n) + 1$ is composite.

5. $\gcd(m^4, n^3)$ is equal either to p^3 or p^4.

6. Since $7875 = 3^2 \times 5^3 \times 7$ and $5292 = 2^2 \times 3^3 \times 7^2$, then the results from challenge 2.1 give:
   (a) 63;
   (b) 661 500;
   (c) 6.

7. (a) You just need to consider the number $3 \times 6 \times 9 \times \cdots \times 99$. Think about the contribution from each of these terms to the power of

3 in the prime factorisation of 100!. The answer is 48.

(b) In general, the power of the prime p in the prime factorisation of $n!$ is given by:

$$\sum_k \left\lfloor \frac{n}{p^k} \right\rfloor,$$

where the sum is over all $k \in \mathbb{N}$ such that $p^k \leq n$, and $\lfloor x \rfloor$ denotes the largest integer not exceeding x.

8. Noting that the power of 5 in the prime factorisation of $n!$ never exceeds that of 2, the required number of zeros is simply the power of 5 in the prime factorisation of $n!$, which may be calculated easily by using the answer to part (b) of the last question.

9. First, if $p = q$ then the the statement is clearly true, so let us suppose that $p > q \geq 5$. Since p and q are both odd and $p^2 - q^2 = (p+q)(p-q)$, it follows that $p^2 - q^2$ is a multiple of 4. In order to show what is required you need to prove that at least one of $p + q$ and $p - q$ is a multiple of 4 and at least one of them is a multiple of 3.

10. You might start by looking at the situation for composite n. For example, $2^{15} - 1 = (2^5 - 1)(2^{10} + 2^5 + 1)$. Can you generalise this and hence answer the question?

11. This follows on noting that $n! - 1$ is not divisible by any of the first n positive integers. It thus possesses a prime factor lying strictly between n and $n!$.

12. The power of any prime appearing in the prime factorisation of a square is necessarily even. Therefore, we just need to look for all possible combinations of even powers of the prime factors. For example, if $n = 3^4 \times 7 \times 19^5 \times 37^2$ then the number of squares dividing n is given by $3 \times 1 \times 3 \times 2 = 18$ since 3^4 gives us three possible even powers 3^0, 3^2 and 3^4, and similarly for the other prime factors.

Exercise 3

1. You simply need to note that

$$\frac{1}{7} + \frac{1}{10} + \frac{1}{13} + \frac{1}{16} + \cdots > \frac{1}{7} + \frac{1}{14} + \frac{1}{21} + \frac{1}{28} + \cdots$$

$$= \frac{1}{7}\left(1 + \frac{1}{2} + \frac{1}{3} + \frac{1}{4} + \cdots\right).$$

The result then follows from the divergence of the harmonic series.

2. (a) This is an improper integral, so just a little care is required. Use the fact that for $x \neq 1$ the expression

$$\frac{1 - x^n}{1 - x}$$

gives the sum of the finite geometric series

$$1 + x + x^2 + \cdots + x^{n-1}.$$

(b) The suggested substitution should be enough of a clue to obtain this result.

3. This sum does actually converge. One way of showing that this is the case is to find first the number of double-digit numbers without a 9 in their decimal representation. These are spread over 8 decades, each of which contains exactly 9 such numbers. Similarly, the three-digit numbers without a 9 in their decimal representation are spread over 8 centuries, each of which contains exactly 8×9 such numbers. Continuing in this way, we obtain

$$\sum_{n \in S} \frac{1}{n} < 8 + \frac{8 \times 9}{10} + \frac{8^2 \times 9}{100} + \cdots$$

$$= 8 + 9 \sum_{k=1}^{\infty} \left(\frac{4}{5}\right)^k$$

$$= 44.$$

4. Using the binomial theorem we may obtain

$$\prod_p \left(1 - \frac{1}{p^2}\right)^{-1} = \prod_p \left(1 + \frac{1}{p^2} + \frac{1}{p^4} + \cdots\right).$$

Note that, for any $k \in \mathbb{N}$, the term $\frac{1}{k^2}$ will appear exactly once when the product on the right-hand side is expanded. Furthermore, the expansion will result only in terms of this type. It is therefore true that
$$\sum_{k=1}^{\infty} \frac{1}{k^2} = \prod_{p}\left(1 - \frac{1}{p^2}\right)^{-1}.$$
From result (1.1) on page 6 we know that the left-hand side of the above equality is irrational. However, if there were only finitely many primes then the right-hand side would be rational, resulting in a contradiction.

Exercise 4

1. (a) 49;
   (b) 16;
   (c) 21;
   (d) 96.

2. The integers $n \leq 50$ having exactly six factors are 12, 18, 20, 28, 32, 44, 45 and 50.

3. (a) 2;
   (b) 33.

4. (a) $\pi(50) = 15$ and $\pi\left(\sqrt{50}\right) = 4$.
   (b) Note first that $\pi(m+5) - \pi(m) = 3$ is satisfied by both $m = 1$ and $m = 2$. Now suppose that $\pi(m+5) - \pi(m) = 3$ and $m > 2$. Then there are three primes amongst the set $\{m+1, m+2, m+3, m+4, m+5\}$, no two of which can consecutive integers (2 and 3 are the only two primes that also happen to be consecutive integers). This means that the primes are $m+1$, $m+3$ and $m+5$. We know that exactly one of these integers is divisible by 3. However, since $m > 2$, this integer has to be a composite multiple of 3, which gives us a contradiction. Thus $m = 1$ and $m = 2$ are the only solutions.
   (c) The pairs of twin primes below 100 are (3,5), (5,7), (11,13), (17,19), (29,31), (41,43), (59,61) and (71,73).

5. (a) If 3 is a factor of n then we may write
$$\phi(n) = 3^{k_1}(3-1)p_2^{k_2}(p_2-1)\cdots p_m^{k_m}(p_m-1),$$
for some set of primes $p_2, p_3, \ldots, p_m$, none of which is equal to 3, and some set of non-negative integers $k_1, k_2, \ldots, k_m$. Then
$$\phi(3n) = 3^{k_1+1}(3-1)p_2^{k_2}(p_2-1)\cdots p_m^{k_m}(p_m-1)$$
$$= 3\phi(n).$$
If, on the other hand, $\phi(3n) = 3\phi(n)$ and 3 is not a factor of n,

then
$$\phi(3n) = \phi(3)\phi(n)$$
$$= 3^0(3-1)p_2^{k_2}(p_2-1)\cdots p_m^{k_m}(p_m-1)$$
$$= 2\phi(n),$$

thereby providing a contradiction and hence proving the result.

(b) Assume that $\phi(n) \mid (n-1)$ and $n = p_1^{k_1} p_2^{k_2} \cdots p_m^{k_m}$ where, without loss of generality, $k_1 \geq 2$. Then $p_1 \mid \phi(n)$ and hence $p_1 \mid (n-1)$, which gives a contradiction.

6. With $n = p_1^{k_1} p_2^{k_2} \cdots p_m^{k_m}$, the following facts should be sufficient to obtain the stated result:
   (a) $\sigma(n) = (1 + p_1 + \cdots + p_1^{k_1}) \times \cdots \times (1 + p_m + \cdots + p_m^{k_m})$;
   (b) if $p = 2$ then $1 + p + \cdots + p^k$ is always odd;
   (c) if p is an odd prime then $1 + p + \cdots + p^k$ is odd if, and only if, k is even.

7. (a) An example is $n = 6$.
   (b) Since $2^k - 1$ is prime and σ is multiplicative, we have
   $$\sigma(n) = \sigma(2^{k-1})\sigma(2^k - 1)$$
   $$= \left(\sum_{m=0}^{k-1} 2^m\right)(1 + 2^k - 1)$$
   $$= (2^k - 1)2^k$$
   $$= 2n.$$

The converse is also true; the only even perfect numbers have the form given. See [4] for a proof of this.

Exercise 5

1. (a) $3x^3 + O(x^2)$;
   (b) $3x^3 + O(x^2)$;
   (c) $5x^2 + O(\log x)$;
   (d) $x + O(1)$.

2. We prove and generalise (a) here, and leave you to tackle (b) and (c). For $i \in \{1, 2\}$, $f_i(x) = O(x^2)$ if there exist positive constants a_i and M_i such that $|f_i(x)| \leq M_i x^2$ for all $x \geq a_i$. Now
$$|f_1(x) + f_2(x)| \leq |f_1(x)| + |f_2(x)|$$
$$\leq (M_1 + M_2)x^2$$
for all $x \geq \max\{a_1, a_2\}$, showing that $O(x^2) + O(x^2) = O(x^2)$. In general, $O(f(x)) + O(f(x)) = O(f(x))$.

3. $F(x) = 4x^3 + O(x^2)$, using the well-known result
$$\sum_{k=1}^{n} k^2 = \tfrac{1}{6}n(n+1)(2n+1).$$

4. It is true that $kn = O(n)$ for any fixed k. However, the values of k appearing in the sum on the left-hand side depend on n. The correct result is
$$\sum_{k=1}^{n} kn = n\sum_{k=1}^{n} k = nO(n^2) = O(n^3).$$

5. First, using the suggestion provided in (a) we obtain
$$x^a > \log_b x \quad \Leftrightarrow \quad a \log b > \frac{\log t}{t}.$$

Next, from the result of challenge 3.1 on page 20 it follows that $e^{\sqrt{t}} > \sqrt{t}$ and hence, remembering that $\log x$ is an increasing function, that $\sqrt{t} > \tfrac{1}{2} \log t$. Thus
$$\frac{\log t}{t} < \frac{2\sqrt{t}}{t} = \frac{2}{\sqrt{t}}.$$
The expression on the right tends to zero as t increases without limit, thereby proving the result.

6. Start by noting that

$$\sqrt[x]{x} = e^{\frac{\log x}{x}} = 1 + \frac{\log x}{x} + \frac{1}{2!}\left(\frac{\log x}{x}\right)^2 + \cdots.$$

Therefore

$$x(\sqrt[x]{x} - 1) = \log x + \frac{(\log x)^2}{2x} + \cdots$$
$$= \log x + O\left(\frac{(\log x)^2}{x}\right).$$

Answers and hints to the exercises

Exercise 6

1. If $\mathbb{Z}$ was a group with respect to multiplication then 1 would be the identity. However, there is no $n \in \mathbb{Z}$ such that $2n = 1$, showing that 2 does not have a multiplicative inverse in $\mathbb{Z}$.

2. (a) Show carefully that the four group axioms are satisfied. For example, the identity is $3^0 = 1$ and the inverse of 3^k is 3^{-k}.
   (b) G is a subgroup of $\mathbb{R}\setminus\{0\}$ with respect to multiplication. To see this, note both that G is a group with respect to the same binary operation and that $G \subseteq \mathbb{R}\setminus\{0\}$.

3. (a) $R_{14} = \{1, 3, 5, 9, 11, 13\}$.
   (b) The group table is given in table 3.

$\otimes_{14}$	1	3	5	9	11	13
1	1	3	5	9	11	13
3	3	9	1	13	5	11
5	5	1	11	3	13	9
9	9	13	3	11	1	5
11	11	5	13	1	9	3
13	13	11	9	5	3	1

Table 3

(c) Table 4 on the current page summarises the situation.

element	order	inverse
1	1	1
3	6	5
5	6	3
9	3	11
11	3	9
13	2	13

Table 4

(d) The subgroups are $\{1\}$, $\{1, 13\}$, $\{1, 9, 11\}$ and $\{1, 3, 5, 9, 11, 13\}$.

4. Table 5 shows the group table of G. The orders of 0, 1, 2 and 3 are 1, 4, 2 and 4, respectively.

$\oplus_4$	0	1	2	3
0	0	1	2	3
1	1	2	3	0
2	2	3	0	1
3	3	0	1	2

Table 5

5. The orders of e, f, g, h, i and j are 1, 2, 2, 3, 3, 2, respectively.

6. Let $x, y \in G$ such that $x^2 = y^2 = e$. Since G is abelian, we have

$$(xy)^2 = xyxy = x^2 y^2 = ee = e,$$

showing that H is closed. Associativity in H follows from that in G. The identity is in H since $e^2 = e$. Finally, if $x \in G$ such that $x^2 = e$, then

$$\begin{aligned} e &= e^2 \\ &= (xx^{-1})(xx^{-1}) \\ &= x^2(x^{-1})^2 \\ &= (x^{-1})^2. \end{aligned}$$

Thus $x^{-1} \in H$, telling us that H is a subgroup of G.

7. First, from the definition of $o(a)$, it is clear that the elements of the set $H = \{e, a, a^2, \ldots, a^{o(a)-1}\}$ are all distinct, and therefore H has $o(a)$ elements. We have closure since for any $n, m \in \{0, 1, 2, \ldots, o(a) - 1\}$ there exist $k, r \in \mathbb{Z}$ with $0 \leq r < o(a)$ such that $a^n a^m = a^{n+m} = a^{o(a)k+r} = a^r$. Associativity follows from that of G. Finally, the identity e is in H and the inverse of a^m is $a^{o(a)-m}$, which is in H.

8. You will see that this question is strongly linked to the previous one.

9. By definition, $o(a^m)$ is the smallest positive integer k such that $(a^m)^k = e$. We know, by theorem 6.5, that $o(a) \mid mk$, so we are looking for the smallest k that satisfies this. However, this minimum value occurs precisely when

$$k = \frac{o(a)}{\gcd(m, o(a))},$$

as required.

10. (a) G is the set of all invertible 2×2 matrices with entries in $\mathbb{R}$. Consider the product of two matrices in G:

$$\begin{pmatrix} a & b \\ c & d \end{pmatrix} \begin{pmatrix} e & f \\ g & h \end{pmatrix} = \begin{pmatrix} ae + bg & af + bh \\ ce + dg & cf + dh \end{pmatrix}.$$

The operation is closed since

$$(ae + bg)(cf + dh) - (af + bh)(ce + dg) = (ad - bc)(eh - gf)$$
$$\neq 0.$$

Next, matrix multiplication is associative. The identity is

$$\begin{pmatrix} 1 & 0 \\ 0 & 1 \end{pmatrix},$$

which is in G, and the inverse of

$$\begin{pmatrix} a & b \\ c & d \end{pmatrix}$$

is

$$\frac{1}{ad - bc} \begin{pmatrix} d & -b \\ -c & a \end{pmatrix},$$

which is also an element of G.

The group is non-commutative since, for example,

$$\begin{pmatrix} 2 & 1 \\ 1 & 1 \end{pmatrix} \begin{pmatrix} 2 & 0 \\ 1 & 1 \end{pmatrix} \neq \begin{pmatrix} 2 & 0 \\ 1 & 1 \end{pmatrix} \begin{pmatrix} 2 & 1 \\ 1 & 1 \end{pmatrix}.$$

(b) Here is a finite subgroup of G with exactly 4 elements:

$$\left\{ \begin{pmatrix} 1 & 0 \\ 0 & 1 \end{pmatrix}, \begin{pmatrix} -1 & 0 \\ 0 & 1 \end{pmatrix}, \begin{pmatrix} 1 & 0 \\ 0 & -1 \end{pmatrix}, \begin{pmatrix} -1 & 0 \\ 0 & -1 \end{pmatrix} \right\}.$$

(c) An infinite subgroup of G is given by:
$$\left\{ \begin{pmatrix} \cos\theta & \sin\theta \\ -\sin\theta & \cos\theta \end{pmatrix} : 0 \le \theta < 2\pi \right\}.$$

(d) We may adapt the above to obtain a finite subgroup of G with exactly n elements:
$$\left\{ \begin{pmatrix} \cos\frac{2\pi k}{n} & \sin\frac{2\pi k}{n} \\ -\sin\frac{2\pi k}{n} & \cos\frac{2\pi k}{n} \end{pmatrix} : 0 \le k \le n-1 \right\}.$$

(e) An example of an infinite subgroup of G in which every element has finite order is:
$$\left\{ \begin{pmatrix} \cos\pi q & \sin\pi q \\ -\sin\pi q & \cos\pi q \end{pmatrix} : q \in \mathbb{Q} \right\}.$$

(f) Finally, we give an infinite subgroup of G in which every non-identity element does not have finite order:
$$\left\{ \begin{pmatrix} 1 & a \\ 0 & 1 \end{pmatrix} : a \in \mathbb{R}, a \ge 0 \right\}.$$

Exercise 7

1. Although somewhat routine calculations, these are nonetheless worth going through at least once in your life.

2. We have $\omega^{23} = \omega^2(\omega^3)^7 = \omega^2$ and $\frac{1}{\omega^{23}} = \omega^{-23} = \omega(\omega^3)^{-8} = \omega$.

3. (a) 1;
   (b) 1;
   (c) 2^k;
   (d) ω^3.

4. All the subgroups will be cyclic, so you just need to have a method for identifying potential generators.

5. (a) This may be proved by induction, noting that
$$|(a+bi)(c+di)|$$
$$= \sqrt{(ac-bd)^2 + (ad+bc)^2}$$
$$= \sqrt{(ac)^2 - 2abcd + (bd)^2 + (ad)^2 + 2abcd + (bc)^2}$$
$$= \sqrt{(a^2+b^2)(c^2+d^2)}$$
$$= |a+bi||c+di|.$$

   (b) Since $z^n = 1$, we have $1 = |z^n| = |z|^n$, from which it follows that $|z| = 1$ (noting that $|z|$ is, by definition, a non-negative real number).

6. Let $\omega = \cos\frac{2\pi}{n} + i\sin\frac{2\pi}{n}$. Then the nth roots of unity are given by $1, \omega, \omega^2, \ldots, \omega^{n-1}$. Now, using the formula for the sum of a finite geometric progression, we obtain
$$1 + \omega + \omega^2 + \ldots + \omega^{n-1} = \frac{\omega^n - 1}{\omega - 1} = 0,$$
bearing in mind that $\omega \neq 1$ for $n \geq 2$.

Exercise 9

1. This is another one of those tasks that, despite being rather straightforward, is worth carrying out in order to gain further appreciation of the structure.

2. You can use $\{3, 11\}$, for example, as a set of generators. The orders of 3 and 11 are 4 and 2, respectively. If f is a character, then we may assign $1, i, -1$ or $-i$ to $f(3)$, and 1 or -1 to $f(11)$.

3. From the definition of $\chi(n)$, its periodicity and result (9.4), it follows that
$$\sum_{n=i}^{j} \chi(n) = \sum_{a \in S_k} \chi(a),$$
where, as the notation implies, the right-hand sum is over some subset S_k of R_k. From result (9.4) we know that
$$\sum_{a \in S_k} \chi(a) = -\sum_{a \in R_k \setminus S_k} \chi(a),$$
and hence
$$\left| \sum_{a \in S_k} \chi(a) \right| = \left| \sum_{a \in R_k \setminus S_k} \chi(a) \right|,$$
with $R_k \setminus S_k$ (known as the *difference* between R_k and S_k) denoting the elements of R_k that remain after those belonging to S_k have been removed. Since R_k contains exactly $\phi(k)$ elements, it must be the case that either S_k or $R_k \setminus S_k$ contains no more that $\frac{1}{2}\phi(k)$ elements. Then, noting that $|\chi(a)| = 1$ for each $a \in R_k$, the result follows from the above equality in conjunction with the triangle inequality 7.2.

4. (a) It can be seen from the character table of the group $(R_{12}, \otimes_{12})$ (see table 8.1 on page 59) that the principal character gives rise to a Dirichlet character with period 6.
   (b) This result is in fact true for any arithmetic function $g(n)$ (and thus in particular for χ_f). We illustrate how this works by way of an example, and leave you to provide a general proof. Suppose that g has period 12 and that it also has period 8. We show that there exists some $m < 8$ such that m is a factor of

12 and g has period m. Note that, since g has period 8, we have $g(1) = g(9) = g(17) = g(25) = \cdots$. As g has period 12, this gives $g(1) = g(5) = g(9)$. Similarly $g(2) = g(6) = g(10)$, $g(3) = g(7) = g(11)$ and $g(4) = g(8) = g(12)$. Thus g has period 4. Of course, this might not be the smallest period of g, but repeated use of the above argument tells us that the smallest period is a factor of 12.

(c) Let $k \in \mathbb{N}$ be such that k is square-free and $k \geq 2$. First, if $k = p$ for some prime p then from (b) above we know that k is the smallest period of χ_f (noting that χ_f cannot have period 1 when $k \geq 2$ since $\chi_f(1) = 1$ and $\chi_f(k) = 0$). We go one step further here in order to prove that k is the smallest period of χ_f for the special case in which k is the product of two primes, p and q. We leave the proof of the general case for you to figure out.
From (b) we know that if χ_f does have a smaller period than k then it is either p or q. Let us assume, without loss of generality, that the smallest period of k is p. Then we must have

$$1 = \chi_f(1) = \chi_f(p+1) = \chi_f(2p+1) = \cdots = \chi_f((q-1)p+1).$$

Let us now consider the set

$$S = \{1, p+1, 2p+1, \ldots, (q-1)p+1\}$$

consisting of q elements. These are all distinct modulo q since, if $ip + 1 \equiv jp + 1 \pmod{q}$ for some $0 \leq i, j \leq q-1$, then, as $\gcd(p, q) = 1$, it follows that $i = j$. Therefore exactly one element of S, $rp + 1$ say, is divisible by q. This implies that $\gcd(k, rp+1) > 1$ and hence that $\chi_f(rp+1) = 0$, giving us a contradiction.

Exercise 10

1. (a) For any $m \in \mathbb{N}$, $\chi_2(3m-2) = 1$, $\chi_2(3m-1) = -1$ and $\chi_2(3m) = 0$.
   (b) We may obtain the result

$$L_2 = \sum_{n=1}^{\infty} \frac{\chi_2(n)}{n}$$
$$= \sum_{k=1}^{\infty} \left(\frac{1}{3k-2} - \frac{1}{3k-1} \right)$$
$$= \int_0^1 \frac{1-x}{1-x^3} dx$$
$$= \int_0^1 \frac{1}{1+x+x^2} dx$$
$$= \frac{\pi}{3\sqrt{3}}.$$

2. (a) The nth term is

$$u_n = \frac{3(5^n - 1)}{5^n}.$$

   (b) For any fixed $\epsilon > 0$, $|u_p - u_q| < \epsilon$ when $p, q > \frac{\log(\frac{3}{\epsilon})}{\log 5}$.

3. (a) The three non-principal Dirichlet characters of $(R_5, \otimes_5)$ are given in table 6.

n	$f_2(n)$	$f_3(n)$	$f_4(n)$
1	1	1	1
2	-1	i	$-i$
3	-1	$-i$	i
4	1	-1	-1

Table 6

(b) We have

$$L_2 = \sum_{k=1}^{\infty} \left(\frac{1}{5k-4} - \frac{1}{5k-3} - \frac{1}{5k-2} + \frac{1}{5k-1} \right)$$

$$= \int_0^1 \frac{(1-x)^2(1+x)}{1-x^5} dx$$

$$= \frac{1}{\sqrt{5}} \log \left(\frac{3+\sqrt{5}}{2} \right)$$

$$= \frac{2}{\sqrt{5}} \coth^{-1} \sqrt{5},$$

$$L_3 = \sum_{k=1}^{\infty} \left(\frac{1}{5k-4} - \frac{1}{5k-1} \right) + i \sum_{k=1}^{\infty} \left(\frac{1}{5k-3} - \frac{1}{5k-2} \right)$$

$$= \int_0^1 \frac{1-x^3}{1-x^5} dx + i \int_0^1 \frac{x(1-x)}{1-x^5} dx$$

$$= \frac{\pi}{5\sqrt{5}} \left(\sqrt{5+2\sqrt{5}} + i\sqrt{5-2\sqrt{5}} \right),$$

$$= \frac{\pi}{5} \left(\cot \frac{\pi}{5} + i \cot \frac{2\pi}{5} \right)$$

and

$$L_4 = \sum_{k=1}^{\infty} \left(\frac{1}{5k-4} - \frac{1}{5k-1} \right) - i \sum_{k=1}^{\infty} \left(\frac{1}{5k-3} - \frac{1}{5k-2} \right)$$

$$= \int_0^1 \frac{1-x^3}{1-x^5} dx - i \int_0^1 \frac{x(1-x)}{1-x^5} dx$$

$$= \frac{\pi}{5\sqrt{5}} \left(\sqrt{5+2\sqrt{5}} - i\sqrt{5-2\sqrt{5}} \right)$$

$$= \frac{\pi}{5} \left(\cot \frac{\pi}{5} - i \cot \frac{2\pi}{5} \right).$$

As a hint for carrying out the integration steps, we may use partial fractions by way of the factorisation

$$1 + x + x^2 + x^3 + x^4$$
$$= \left(x^2 - 2x \cos \frac{2\pi}{5} + 1 \right) \left(x^2 + 2x \cos \frac{\pi}{5} + 1 \right).$$

Exercise 11

1. (a) 0;
   (b) −1;
   (c) 0.

2. First, $\mu(1!) = 1$, $\mu(2!) = -1$ and $\mu(3!) = 1$. Next, note that $4 = 2^2$ is a factor of $n!$ for all $n \geq 4$, so that $\mu(n!) = 0$ when $n \geq 4$.

3. (a) $\log 858$;
   (b) $\log 15$;
   (c) $\log 108$.

4. Since $\Lambda(2)\Lambda(3) = \log 2 \times \log 3 \neq 0 = \Lambda(2 \times 3)$, for example, we see that the Mangoldt function is not multiplicative.

5. (a) 12;
   (b) 13;
   (c) 58.

6. The smallest possible value of x for which the inequality is true is 8.

7. (a) For suitable values of n, each expression could be equal to any of 1, 0 or −1. For example, $\mu(1 \times 2) = -1$, $\mu(2 \times 3) = 1$ and $\mu(3 \times 4) = 0$, while $\mu(1 \times 3) = -1$, $\mu(2 \times 4) = 0$ and $\mu(3 \times 5) = 1$.
   (b) One of n, $n+1$, $n+2$ or $n+3$ is a multiple of $4 = 2^2$.

8. $\Lambda(2!) = \log 2$ and $\Lambda(n!) = 0$ for all other values of n.

9. For example, $\mu(3 \times 6) = \mu(18) = 0 \neq -1 = \mu(3)\mu(6)$.

10. (a) From the definition of τ, it is the case that

$$\tau(n) = \sum_{d|n} f(d),$$

where f is the arithmetic function given by $f(n) = 1$ for all $n \in \mathbb{N}$. Then, using the Möbius inversion formula (11.2), we

obtain
$$1 = f(n) = \sum_{d|n} \mu(d) \tau\left(\frac{n}{d}\right).$$

The first result follows since d and $\frac{n}{d}$ may be interchanged without altering the value of the sum.

The second result may be obtained in a similar manner, noting that
$$\sigma(n) = \sum_{d|n} d.$$

(b) With $n = 6$,

$$\sum_{d|6} \mu\left(\frac{6}{d}\right) \tau(d) = \mu(6)\tau(1) + \mu(3)\tau(2) + \mu(2)\tau(3) + \mu(1)\tau(6)$$
$$= 1 - 2 - 2 + 4$$
$$= 1$$

and

$$\sum_{d|6} \mu\left(\frac{6}{d}\right) \sigma(d) = \mu(6)\sigma(1) + \mu(3)\sigma(2) + \mu(2)\sigma(3) + \mu(1)\sigma(6)$$
$$= 1 - 3 - 4 + 12$$
$$= 6.$$

11. If n is square-free then
$$\sum_{d^2|n} \mu(d) = \mu(1) = 1.$$

Furthermore, $\mu(n) = 1$ or $\mu(n) = -1$, depending on whether n has an even or an odd number of prime factors, respectively. Either way, $\{\mu(n)\}^2 = 1$.

Now assume that n is not square-free. Then we may write $n = m^2 k$ for some $m \geq 2$ and square-free k. Therefore
$$\sum_{d^2|n} \mu(d) = \sum_{d|m} \mu(d) = 0,$$

where in the last step we used result (11.1). Also, since n is not square free, it follows that
$$\{\mu(n)\}^2 = 0.$$

Exercise 12

1. This calculation proceeds as follows:

$$f(6) = \sum_{d|6} \phi(d)\sigma\left(\frac{6}{d}\right)$$
$$= \phi(1)\sigma(6) + \phi(2)\sigma(3) + \phi(3)\sigma(2) + \phi(6)\sigma(1)$$
$$= 12 + 4 + 6 + 2$$
$$= 24.$$

2. Table 7 gives the Dirichet inverse of $\sigma(n)$ from $n = 1$ to $n = 8$.

n	$\sigma(n)$	$\sigma^{-1}(n)$
1	1	1
2	3	-3
3	4	-4
4	7	2
5	6	-6
6	12	12
7	8	-8
8	15	0

Table 7

3. Let $f(n) = g(n) = n^2$. Then f and g are both completely multiplicative functions. We have

$$(f*g)(4) = \sum_{d|4} d^2 \left(\frac{4}{d}\right)^2 = \sum_{d|4} 4^2 = 48$$

and

$$(f*g)(2) = \sum_{d|2} d^2 \left(\frac{2}{d}\right)^2 = \sum_{d|2} 2^2 = 8.$$

Since $(f*g)(4) \neq (f*g)(2)(f*g)(2)$, we see that $f*g$ is not completely multiplicative.

4. The calculation goes as follows:

$$(f \circ G)(\pi) = \sum_{n \leq \pi} \sigma(n) \cos \frac{\pi}{n}$$

$$= \sigma(1) \cos \pi + \sigma(2) \cos \frac{\pi}{2} + \sigma(3) \cos \frac{\pi}{3}$$

$$= -1 + 0 + 2$$

$$= 1.$$

5. We have

$$(f \circ G)(x) = \sum_{n \leq x} 2n \left(\frac{x+1}{n} \right)$$

$$= \sum_{n \leq x} 2(x+1)$$

$$= 2\lfloor x \rfloor (x+1).$$

6. You will find that

$$\phi^{-1}(n) = \sum_{d \mid n} d\mu(d)$$

for $n = 1$ to $n = 6$. The above relation is in fact true for any $n \in \mathbb{N}$, and you ought to try to prove that this is the case.

Exercise 14

1. On using the 'rectangles trick' (after noting that $\frac{2\log t}{t^2}$ is a decreasing function for $t \geq 2$) it may be seen that

$$\frac{2\log 3}{3^2} + \frac{2\log 4}{4^2} + \cdots < 2\int_2^\infty \frac{\log t}{t^2}\,dt.$$

Therefore

$$\frac{2\log 2}{2^2} + \frac{2\log 3}{3^2} + \frac{2\log 4}{4^2} + \cdots < \frac{2\log 2}{2^2} + 2\int_2^\infty \frac{\log t}{t^2}\,dt,$$

and the result follows.

2. Asymptotic formulae are given by:

$$\sum_{n\leq x} \frac{1}{\sqrt{n}} = 2\sqrt{x} + O(1)$$

and

$$\sum_{n\leq x} n\log n = \frac{x^2}{4}(2\log x - 1) + O(x\log x).$$

3. From result (14.1) we may infer that

$$\frac{\sum_{p\leq x} \frac{\log p}{p}}{\log x} \to 1 \quad \text{as} \quad x \to \infty,$$

and hence that the relative error in using this approximation tends to zero as x increases without limit. On the other hand, although result (14.1) implies that the absolute error is bounded, it does not provide us with information on the maximum value of this error. I used *Mathematica*® to obtain the numerical result

$$\left|\sum_{p\leq x} \frac{\log p}{p} - \log x\right| < 1.34$$

for all $x \in \mathbb{R}$ such that $2 \leq x \leq 50\,000$. I also carried out some spot checks on a number of narrower intervals containing much larger values of x, and in none of these cases was the absolute error greater than 1.34. However, such numerical results merely indicate a possible upper bound on the absolute error rather than provide any cast-iron proof that this is indeed a genuine upper bound.

Answers and hints to the exercises

4. Yes, it is in fact true that
$$\frac{(\log t)^n}{t} \to 0 \quad \text{as} \quad t \to \infty$$
for any given $n \in \mathbb{N}$. To show that this is the case, we may adopt a similar approach to that used in answering question 5 in exercise 5 (see page 193). Let us fix $n \in \mathbb{N}$. From the result of challenge 3.1 on page 20 it follows that $\exp t^{\frac{1}{n+1}} > t^{\frac{1}{n+1}}$. Thus, remembering once more that $\log x$ is an increasing function, we obtain
$$t^{\frac{1}{n+1}} > \frac{1}{n+1} \log t$$
and hence
$$t^{\frac{n}{n+1}} > \left(\frac{1}{n+1} \log t\right)^n.$$
This may be rearranged to give
$$\frac{(\log t)^n}{t} < (n+1)^n t^{-\frac{1}{n+1}},$$
from which the result follows.

Bibliography

Books

[1] T. M. Apostol. *Introduction to Analytic Number Theory.* Springer, 1976.

[2] P. B. Bhattacharya, S. K. Jain, and S. R. Nagpaul. *Basic Abstract Algebra.* Second. Cambridge University Press, 1994.

[3] C. J. Bradley. *Introduction to Number Theory.* UKMT, 2010. ISBN: 978-1-906001-12-4.

[4] D. M. Burton. *Elementary Number Theory.* McGraw-Hill, 1998.

[5] J. Derbyshire. *Prime Obsession. Bernhard Riemann and the Greatest Unsolved Problem in Mathematics.* John Henry Press, 2003.

[6] Martin Griffiths. *The Backbone of Pascal's Triangle.* UKMT, 2008. ISBN: 978-1-906001-04-9.

[7] R. Haggarty. *Fundamentals of Mathematical Analysis.* Addison-Wesley, 1989.

[8] G. H. Hardy and E. M. Wright. *An Introduction to the Theory of Numbers.* Sixth. Oxford University Press, 2008.

[9] L. Kronecker. *G. Lejeune Dirichlet's Werke.* American Mathematical Society, 1969.

[10] H. A. Priestley. *Introduction to Complex Analysis.* Second. Oxford University Press, 2003.

[11] H. E. Rose. *A Course in Number Theory.* Second. Oxford University Press, 1994.

[12] W. J. Le Veque. *Topics in Number Theory.* 2 volumes. Dover, 2002.

Articles and other materials

[13] Robin Chapman. "Evaluating $\zeta(2)$". 2003. URL: http://empslocal.ex.ac.uk/people/staff/rjchapma/etc/zeta2.pdf.

[14] Pete L. Clark. "Dirichlet's theorem on primes in arithmetic progression". Math 4400/6400 — Number Theory. 2009.
URL: http://www.math.uga.edu/~pete/4400DT.pdf.

[15] L. Euler. "Variae observationes circa series infinitas". Mathematical Association of America: The Euler Archive E72. In: *Commentarii academiae scientiarum Petropolitanae* 9 (1744), pp. 160–188.
URL: http://eulerarchive.maa.org/pages/E072.html.

[16] Ben Green and Terence Tao.
"The primes contain arbitrarily long arithmetic progressions".
In: (2004). arXiv:math/0404188v6.
URL: http://arxiv.org/abs/math/0404188v6.

[17] S. Gueron and R. Tessler. "Infinitely many primes in arithmetic progressions. the cyclotomic polynomial method".
In: *The Mathematical Gazette* 86.505 (2002), pp. 110–114.

[18] H. N. Shapiro. "On primes in arithmetic progression".
In: *Annals of Mathematics* 52 (1950), pp. 231–243.

[19] Jerry Shurman. "Dirichlet's problem on the disk". Course materials for Mathematics 311: Complex Analysis. 2012.
URL: http://people.reed.edu/~jerry/311/dirichletap.pdf.

[20] Kuat Yessenov. "Dirichlet's theorem on primes in arithmetic progression". Course project. 2008. URL:
http://people.csail.mit.edu/kuat/courses/dirichlet.pdf.

Web sites

[21] John J O'Connor and Edmund F Robertson.
Johann Peter Gustav Lejeune Dirichlet. 2000.
URL: http://www-history.mcs.st-andrews.ac.uk/Mathematicians/Dirichlet.html.

[22] John J O'Connor and Edmund F Robertson.
The MacTutor History of Mathematics archive. 2012.
URL: http://www-history.mcs.st-and.ac.uk/.

[23] Eric W. Weisstein. *Cyclotomic Polynomial.* From MathWorld–A Wolfram Web Resource. 2012. URL: http://mathworld.wolfram.com/CyclotomicPolynomial.html.

[24] Wikipedia. *Fundamental theorem of algebra.* 2012. URL: http://en.wikipedia.org/w/index.php?title=Fundamental_theorem_of_algebra&oldid=491771083.

[25] Wikipedia. *Light's associativity test.* 2012. URL: http://en.wikipedia.org/w/index.php?title=Light%27s_associativity_test&oldid=488746862.

[26] Wikipedia. *Linnik's theorem.* 2012. URL: http://en.wikipedia.org/w/index.php?title=Linnik%27s_theorem&oldid=491153293.

[27] Wikipedia. *Primes in arithmetic progression.* 2012. URL: http://en.wikipedia.org/w/index.php?title=Primes_in_arithmetic_progression&oldid=481647452.

Index

abelian group, 46
Algebra, Fundamental Theorem of
  ∼, 57
algebraically closed, 57
argument, 166
arithmetic
  ∼ function, 25
  modular ∼, 161
Arithmetic, Fundamental Theorem
  of ∼, 11
associativity, 43
associativity test
  Light's ∼, 178
asymptotic relation, 38

bounded, 154

Cartesian form, 166
Cauchy
  ∼ convergence criterion, 154
  ∼ sequence, 154
Cayley table, 48
character, 59, 60
  ∼ table, 60
  complex-valued ∼, 136
  Dirichlet ∼, 70
  principal Dirichlet ∼, 71
  real-valued ∼, 130
closed, algebraically ∼, 57
closure, 43
commutative, 46

completely multiplicative, 28
complex conjugate, 165
complex-valued character, 136
congruent, 161
conjugate, complex ∼, 165
contradiction, proof by ∼, 5
convergence, 153
  Cauchy ∼ criterion, 154
convolution
  Dirichlet ∼, 91
  generalised ∼, 95
cyclic, 51
cyclotomic polynomial, 147

De Moivre's theorem, 167
decomposition, prime ∼, 11
difference, 200
Dirichlet
  ∼ character, 70
  ∼ convolution, 91
  ∼ inverse, 94
  ∼ L-functions, 75
  ∼ product, 91
  principal ∼ character, 71
divergence, 153
divisor, greatest common ∼, 13

elliptic curves, 148
Euler's
  ∼ phi-function, 29
  ∼ theorem, 147

Euler-Fermat theorem, 147
exponential series, 157

factor, highest common ∼, 13
factorisation, prime ∼, 11
factors
    number of ∼, 26
    sum of the ∼, 27
finite group, 47
floor function, 88
form
    Cartesian ∼, 166
    modulus-argument ∼, 166
function
    arithmetic ∼, 25
    floor ∼, 88
    Möbius ∼, 83
    Mangoldt ∼, 86
    multiplicative ∼, 28
    Riemann zeta ∼, 145
    step ∼, 31
Fundamental Theorem of
    ∼ Algebra, 57
    ∼ Arithmetic, 11

generalised
    ∼ Möbius inversion formula, 98
    ∼ convolution, 95
generators, 50
greatest common divisor, 13
Gregory's series, 77
group, 44
    ∼ table, 48
    abelian ∼, 46
    finite ∼, 47

harmonic
    ∼ number, 17
    ∼ series, 18, 157
Hasse's Principle, 148
highest common factor, 13

identity, 44
inequality, triangle ∼, 56
interchanging the order of summation, 169
inverse, 44
    Dirichlet ∼, 94
    multiplicative ∼, 163
inversion formula
    generalised Möbius ∼, 98
    Möbius ∼, 84
isomorphic, 50

L-functions, Dirichlet ∼, 75
Lagrange's theorem, 50
Latin square, 48
Light's associativity test, 178
limit, 154
logarithm, natural ∼, 7

Möbius
    ∼ function, 83
    ∼ inversion formula, 84
    generalised ∼ inversion formula, 98
Mangoldt function, 86
modular arithmetic, 161
modulo, 161
modulus, 166
modulus-argument form, 166
monotone, 154
multiplicative
    ∼ function, 28
    ∼ inverse, 163
    ∼ notation, 45
    ∼ property, 60
    completely ∼, 28

number
    ∼ of factors, 26
    harmonic ∼, 17
    perfect ∼, 33

order, 47, 49

Index

orthogonality relation, 66

perfect number, 33
phi-function, Euler's ∼, 29
polynomial, cyclotomic ∼, 147
prime
    ∼ decomposition, 11
    ∼ factorisation, 11
    ∼ number theorem, 145
    twin ∼, 32
principal Dirichlet character, 71
product, Dirichlet ∼, 91
proof by contradiction, 5

quadratic residue, 147
quotient, 161

real-valued character, 130
relation, 50
    asymptotic ∼, 38
    orthogonality ∼, 66
remainder, 161
residue
    ∼ classes, 48
    quadratic ∼, 147
Riemann zeta function, 145
roots of unity, 53

sequence, Cauchy ∼, 154
series
    exponential ∼, 157
    Gregory's ∼, 77
    harmonic ∼, 18, 157
square-free, 73
step function, 31
subgroup, 47
sum of the factors, 27

table
    Cayley ∼, 48
    character ∼, 60
    group ∼, 48
theorem
    De Moivre's ∼, 167
    Euler's ∼, 147
    Euler-Fermat ∼, 147
    Lagrange's ∼, 50
    prime number ∼, 145
totient function, 29
triangle inequality, 56
twin prime, 32

unity, roots of ∼, 53

zeta, Riemann ∼ function, 145